TRADITIONAL CRAFTS OF ASSAM

Development Dynamics through Touristic Marketing

Mrinmoy K. Sarma

Maulana Abul Kalam Azad Institute of Asian Studies,
Kolkata

ANSHAH Anshah Publishing House

ISBN: 978-81-8364-048-0

Published in 2008

Traditional Crafts of Assam

Published by:
Anshah Publishing House, Delhi
Sales Office: 115-A, Vikas Marg, Shakarpur, Delhi-110092
Ph.: 9810522367, 22500954

To

My PARENTS –

Srijut Dr Kailash Ch. Sarma

And

Srijuta Renuka Sarma

Who are my inspirations, and my idols…

Acknowledgements

I acknowledge with gratefulness the support in the form of the Research Fellowship received from Maulana Abul Kalam Azad Institute of Asian Studies (MAKAIAS), Kolkata. They have been very generous in extending the deadline for submission of the work due to my personal engagements outside the country. I am thankful to the Institute.

I take this opportunity to thank the Tezpur University authority for allowing me to undertake this study.

I am grateful to Sri Umesh Patir, Sri Tarun Borah, Sri Uttam Baruah and Ms Tasmira Ahmed who helped me in completing the work. My deepest thanks go to my wife Santirekha Chowdhury (Sarma) and my little daughter Srutisree for bearing with me during the tough period of the research work.

Practicing Tour Operators, and the policy makers like the State Government and the North East Council (NEC) can take note of the findings of this study and might like to implement the suggestions and recommendations.

My drudgery will bear fruit if the economically poor but artistically richest of the rich artisans of my beloved State get benefited, even marginally by the findings of this work.

M. K. Sarma

Contents

List of Maps and Photographic Plates

Maps

Photo Plate

Introduction

Craft has been playing a vital role in the socio-cultural and economic milieu of a society. Hand made products have been a part of a society's culture, and crafts are often treated as authentic for the purity and direct human creativity associated with it. Human expressions take the form of a craft when one cannot indulge in the luxury of spending one's resources in works that do not serve any utilitarian purpose. Thus crafts have been the medium of creativity for the economically repressed ones.

However, crafts cannot be seen as only the mouthpiece of creativity of the oppressed. The silver lining is the tremendous economic importance the craft work itself is attached to. Though the utilitarian angle of the crafts in the recent times has given way to the aesthetic side of it, the values crafts carry have become manifold. Now-a-days crafts are attached with lifestyles of the people residing thousands of miles away from the place where it is being produced. Thanks to globalisation and the newly found lifestyles of the rich and powerful! This entails export of the creative, indigenous and authentic craft works across the continents.

Tourism is invisible export! The tourists come to a destination and spend their money in terms of scarce foreign exchange; hence, the tourists are welcome in most places of the world. They not only come consume the services of the tourism sector or only products of daily needs in a destination. Most of the tourists spend considerable amount of money in shopping. They shop for souvenirs of their visit to the destination, to offer gifts (at depict their visit) to near and dear ones, and yes, of course to "bolster memories" at a distant and future time. To do so they look for products authentic to the destination that are pure and unique to it only. Researches have found that the tourists' first preference in such a pursuit is the craft work of the host region. They buy the crafts and buy in huge volume (in monetary terms).

Many tourists roam around with an intention of visiting beautiful craft producing regions around the world. They like to experience the creative vistas the craftsmen go through; see for themselves the economic and social conditions of those weavers or wood carvers or potters whose artistic expressions are so marvelous. This is termed as Craft Tourism in modern tourism vocabulary.

Assam, the heartland of the whole of North East India is a colourful mosaic of various craft traditions. Being the abode of two most fertile valleys across the entire NE India, Assam has been attracting migrations since thousands of years. This makes the State a melting pot of diverse cultures, ethnicity, habits, skills, and more than anything else humanity. This has given rise to diversity in the tradition and social life of the State. In the process, different mind blowing creative forms like languages, dialects, songs, dances and tangible works like the crafts have taken birth. These forms are taken care of by the benevolent natural environment of the region to make them grow into full fledged mature forms. Thus Assam has a variety that is being reared by the jealous guardians of these cultures and traditions.

Therefore, the alternative tourists who are looking for something new might very well be exposed to this mind boggling huge ground of multi-culturism. With this aim in mind the present study was conceived way back in 2004.

Assam, being one of the most underdeveloped States of India (itself suffering from malnourishment) bears promises of development only in labour intensive sectors. Three such promising sectors suitable for a State like Assam are sericulture, agriculture and tourism. The State must try to adopt all these three with renewed interest so that overall development can be achieved. Tourism and sericulture in the form of craft works are tried to be linked with each other. It is heartening to note that both the sectors have the potentiality to complement each other, and growth in one sector will surely help in the progress of the other sector. If Assam become more famous in hand-made natural textile (product of sericulture) it can promote alternative tourism as more tourists will be interested in witnessing such a famous work. More tourists visiting the State means more will be the exposure of the craft sectors, and more famous they will become. The following simple causal loop diagram will help in explaining the relationship between these two sectors.

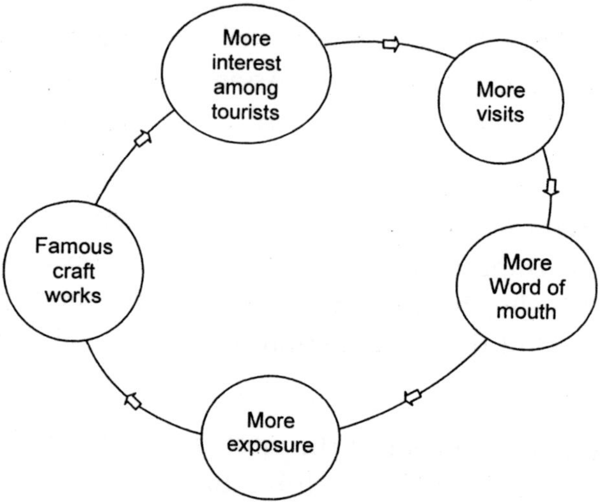

All these reasons played the catalysts for initiating this work. The work simply explores the possibility of offering the craft works for touristic exposure so that a comprehensive future plan can be chalked out.

However, it must be noted here that it is not a comprehensive and exhaustive work on the crafts of the State. It only tries to expose the most prominent craft concentration so that the same could be offered for tourist consumption. The traditional pockets are only taken into account and hence the newly developed craft areas like craft villages and commercial hubs are not given prime importance.

1

Tourism and Attractions in Assam

TOURISM

Travel is an integral part of modern day lifestyle of the world. People have been on the move for various reasons and thus consuming tremendous amount of resources throughout the world.

By and large, it is widely admitted that tourism is one of the few sectors that can bring about a real growth to the economy without creating significant regional or economic disparity. Tourism is also recognised as the most promising industry globally, which possesses tremendous capacity for growth and revenue generation. This industry has already made inroads into the mainstream of the economy of the world. Throughout last few decades tourism has been generating receipts, which were larger than the world trade. According to projections, by the end of the first quarter of this century tourism will have grown at a faster rate than the world's collective wealth!

In 1994, the worldwide tourism industry generated US$ 362.1 billion which increased to US$ 451.4 billion in 1998, and went up to US$ 481.6 billion in 2000. The industry generated US$ 682.7 billion from a total worldwide arrival of 808 million travellers in the year 2005 (UNWTO, 2006). Out of these, almost 90 per cent were generated from domestic tourism. However, in many countries like India, domestic tourism is often understated as keeping records for domestic movement of tourists are sometimes impossible.

The industry contributed 214.7 million jobs up to the year 2003 (WTTC, 2004), which is almost 8.1 per cent of the total available jobs worldwide. This milestone is achieved in spite of global tourism industry suffering a set back in the year 2003 due to the aftermath of the 9-11 incident (UNWTO, 2003-2004). In 2004 almost 10 million (9,931,000) new jobs are estimated to have been created in the tourism sector, out of which 3.3 million jobs are directly related to the industry.

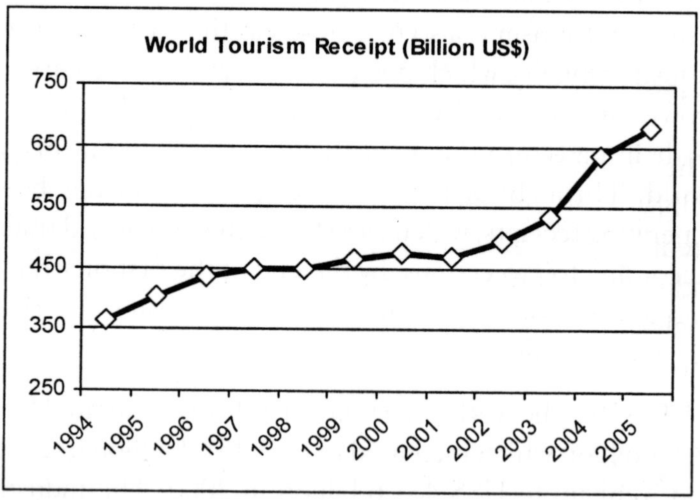

Source: Tourism Market Trends, 2006 Edition-Annex UNWTO.

Very few industries have evolved as rapidly as tourism in the relatively short span of a few decades. Though tourism exists from time immemorial, it attained the status of an organised sector only in the first part of the 20th century, which was propagated by the rapid spurt of economic activities after the World War II. Developed countries, using their huge resource-base to build and modify infrastructure, captured the unprecedented opportunities thrown open by the progress of technology, like commercialisation of international flights during that period. Though developing countries rose to the occasion a little bit later, they soon discovered the potential of tourism and its role in development of economy, and started to invest heavily in this sector. Popularity of this industry went on increasing among the investors as it maintained a steady growth rate throughout the years.

WORLD TOURISM ORGANISATION'S VISION 2020

The United Nations World Tourism Organisation (UNWTO), the apex body on tourism few years back predicted that US $ 2000 billion will be generated by the industry within the year 2020 (Bezbarua, 1999). It has analysed the emerging trends and factors, which will influence the future growth pattern of the industry. Some of the important observations of UNWTO are summarised below:

- By 2020, there will be 1.6 billion international tourist arrivals and tourism receipts will rise to a staggering US$ 2000 billion, globally.

- There will be sustained average annual growth rate of 4.3 per cent (for arrivals) and 6.7 per cent (for receipts) throughout the world till 2020.
- In spite of this growth only 7 per cent of the world's population will become potential tourists. Thus according to WTO the industry would still be in infancy even in the year 2020.
- The top 10 tourist receiving countries would undergo major changes and *China* would be receiving maximum number of tourists (estimated to be 137.1 million with a market share of 8.6%) by 2020. Traditional market leader, France would come down to the third position. China will have an average growth rate of 8.0 per cent in tourist arrivals during the period 1995-2020.
- There will be changes in the top tourist originating countries. Japan, China, and Russian Federation will emerge as the new major outbound tourist countries.
- Though Europe will remain the largest tourist-receiving region, its share will come down to 45 per cent from the present 59 per cent.
- South Asia will grow at a rate of 6.1 per cent per annum during the period but its share will grow only up to 1.2 per cent from the present 0.7 per cent.

INDIA'S SHARE

India, though larger in size and richer in touristic offerings than many of the leading tourist destinations, is responsible for only less than 1 per cent of the total tourism receipt (Sarma, 2003) generated in the world. India received only around 3.54 Million tourists in the year 2004-2005 (FHRAI, 2005). Till the recent time India has been considered a *serious* and *spiritual* destination rather than a destination where one can relax and have fun. (Sarma, 2000). However, this concept is gradually changing with aggressive promotional campaigns taken up by the National Tourism Organisation's (NTOs). As in the case of all developing nations the communication network used by the average traveler in India had been limited to the traditional information sources till the other day. The Internet connectivity was also minimal till the recent times. Hence, the marketers heavily relied upon PR in print and electronic media, printed brochures, fliers, post cards, and formal and informal referrals. Apart from these, the newest trend in the country has been the extensive use of the distribution channel, i.e., the tour and travel operators and agents. Ironically enough, the Indian tourism industry traditionally has not been accustomed in using advertisements unlike their counterparts elsewhere in the globe. Therefore, the visitors are not used to receive messages through advertisements.

Even with modernisation the Indian industry has seen in the recent times, the country's share of the total tourism receipt has been predicted as only 1.2 per cent. This is in spite of the fact that the growth in the Indian industry will be much higher than the global one (while predicting the country's share it is safely assumed that all tourists visiting south Asia will be visiting India too). Whatever small the percentage it is translated to be a whopping US $ 24 billion. In the present exchange rate regime this is Rs. 1,08,000 crore in just a single given year (2020).

TOURISM DEFINED

According to 1991-92 the UNWTO definition, tourism *comprises the activities of persons traveling to and staying in places outside their usual environment for not more than one consecutive year for leisure, business and other purposes.* In UK, the Tourism Society adopted a definition in 1979 based on the work of Burkart and Medlik (Middleton 1994), which in turn draws on earlier definitions and has been widely accepted, which says *tourism is deemed to include any activity concerned with the temporary short-term movement of people to destinations outside the places where they normally live and work, and their activities during the stay at these destinations.* From these two definitions, following characteristics of tourism can be derived—

1. Visitors' activities are concerned only with aspects of life outside normal routines of work and social commitments and outside the location of these routines.
2. The activity necessitates travel, and nearly in every case, some form of transport to the destinations is required.
3. The destination is the focus for a range of activities and a range of facilities are required there to support those activities.

It is clear from the definition that any kind of movement of individuals or group of individuals to a place outside the person(s)' routine movement for day-to-day activities is considered as an activity involved in tourism and the individuals are known as tourists. relaxating, fun seeking, visiting places of attractions.

TOURISM AND ASSAM

The Northeast of India constitutes eight states (officially) of Arunachal Pradesh, Assam, Manipur, Meghalaya, Mizoram, Nagaland, Sikkim and Tripura. Assam is the heartland of Northeast India. It lies between 89° 49' E and 97° 26' E longitudes and between 24°10' N and 27°58' N latitudes. As per 2001 census, the area of Assam is 78,438 sq. km and its total population stood at 2,66,38,407. The State is surrounded by Bhutan and Arunachal Pradesh on the North, Nagaland and Manipur on the East, Meghalaya and Mizoram on the South and Bangladesh, Tripura and West Bengal on the West. Apart from this the borders with Bangladesh and Bhutan share international border with Assam. The terrain of the State can be divided as plains and hills. The plain region can be again sub-divided as the Brahmaputra valley and the Barak valley. The average maximum and minimum temperature of the State is 33°C and 6°C respectively. The official languages of the State are Assamese, Bengali and Bodo. The major crops grown in the State are rice, wheat, jute, coconut, sugarcane, cotton, etc., while the major plantations are Tea and Rubber.

Assam, an embodiment of the natural beauty and grace has many resources to offer to the visitors of different interests. The State has got its own identity due to its unmatched physical and socio-cultural characteristics. The State is fortunate to have ungrudging blessings of the nature. The enchanting hills, dancing rivers, roaring waterfalls, thick and dark forests, innumerable varieties of flora and fauna, countless species of wild animals, melodious folk music, thrilling festivals, variety of delicious dishes, handlooms and handicrafts of the State have made it unique prompting "Incredible India" campaign (of Government of India) to describe Assam as "the Paradise Unexplored" (along with the rest of North East India). The rich mosaic of flora and fauna of the State renders it a spot in the seven hottest bio-diversity hotspots of the world (part of the Indo-Burma region). Further, there are also many historical and religious places of tourists' attraction. These unmatched and unique features of Assam make it a *destined* destination to the travellers from different parts of the globe.

The unique locational advantage of Assam also offers greater opportunity for development of tourism in the State. The State is attached to Myanmar, a gateway to ASEAN countries.

The capital of the State is Guwahati. The city is the gateway to other parts of the Northeast India also and therefore, called "*The Light of the East*". Located at the bank of the river Brahmaputra, the city is a major commercial hub of the Northeast India. It is home to many temples that date back to Vedic times. Devotees from far and near throng the temples daily. The holy places of the Guwahati include the Kamakhya, the Basista Ashram, the Nabagraha Temple, the Ugrata Temple, the Dirgheswari Temple and the Ashwaklanta Temple.

Even with all these resources with tremendous potential, the flow of tourist to the State has been very marginal. The governments at State and central levels have been attaching great importance to the promotion and development of the tourism industry in the State. The silver lining is that the number of tourist inflowing to Assam has been increasing. The table reproduced below shows that the number of domestic and foreign tourists' arrival during last three years has increased tremendously. In the year 2003, the State received domestic tourists numbering 21,56,675 and the number increased to 24,67,652 in the year 2005. Similarly, the inflow of foreign tourists also increased from 6,610 in 2003 to 10,782 in 2005.

A brief review about the tourism resources in Assam is made in the following section:

Table 1.1: Tourist Arrivals in Assam

	Year	*Domestic*	*Foreign*	*Total*
Assam	2003	2156675	6610	2163285
	2004	2288093	7285	2295378
	2005	2467652	10782	2478434

Source: http://164.100.24.219/rsq/quest.asp?qref=115542 retrieved on 30/01/07.

NATURAL RESOURCES

This region's virgin forest and untouched rain forests is the habitat of a great veriety of plants, animals and birds. Some of the species found in The National Parks and Wild Life Sanctuaries are endangered or rarely seen elsewhere in the world. Certain highly endangered bird species (included in the red book of the UNESCO) like *White winged wood duck, Sclater monal, Temminck's tragopan, Bangal florican* are found in the State. One-horned Asiatic Rhinoceros are found only in the Kaziranga National Park of Assam. There are five National Parks in the State. These are Kaziranga, Manas, Nameri, Orang and Dibru-Saikhowa. In addition to these, there are many Wild Life Sanctuaries in the State. Out of all these the follwoing are worth mentioning. They are: Pobitora Wildlife Sanctuary, Sonai Rupai Wildlife Sanctuary, Bura-Chapori Wildlife Sanctuary, Laokhowa Wildlife Sanctuary, Pobha or Milroy Sanctuary, Chakrashila Wildlife Sanctuary, Borṅadi Wildlife Sanctuary, Gorampani Wildlife Sanctuary, Golaghat Gibbon Wildlife Sanctuary, Nambor Wildlife Sanctuary, East Karbi Anglong Wildlife Sanctuary, Karbi Anglong Wildlife Sanctuary, and Panidihing Bird Sanctuary.

The wild animals found in the Parks and Sanctuaries of the State include Asiatic water buffalo, sloth bear, gibbon elephant, golden langurs, wild buffalo, sambher, tiger, wild pig, wild horses, leopard, serow, goral blythe's tragopan, Himalayan black dear, jungle cat, wild dog, marten, the pigmy hog, hillock gibbon, the stamped tailed macaque, golden masher fish, the capped langur, the clouded leopard, the golden cat, etc. The extinct pigmy hogs are found mainly in Manas National Park. Efforts are being made, however, by the Forest Department of Government of Assam to create an artificial habitat for them near the Nameri National Park so that breeding of the pigmy hog could be started in the wild. Pigmy hogs are not found elsewhere in the world.

The State is well known for the pitcher plant (found abundantly only in Meghalaya apart form the State) and several unique varieties of ferns and a spectacular collection of orchids. The state is also famous for its orchids, which are found very commonly here. The forests of the state are rich in valuable and vulnerable trees. Trees like Sal, Teak, Australian Acacia, etc., largely grown in the forests.

RELIGIOUS RESOURCES

Places of worship have been the biggest centers of attraction for pilgrims from several parts of the world and especially from other parts of India. The State Assam has a very rich religious heritage. There are many religious places scattered all over the State, particularly in Guwahati and its surroundings. Devotees from different places throng the religious places daily. The main religious places include the temple of Goddess Kamakhya on the Nilachal hills, Siva temple Umananda situated on the island in the river Brahmaputra, the Navagraha temple, Basistha Ashram and

Balaji temple of Guwahati; Mahabhairab temple and Bhairabi of Tezpur; Hayagrib Madhab Temple of Hajo, etc. The Kamakhya is one of the most revered shrines of the Hindu faith. The shrine finds mention in the inscription of King Samudragupta's pillar at Allahabad. In the month of June Ambubachi mela is celebrates in this temple. Thousands of devotees from different places of India throng the temple. Another well known religious place is the Poa-Mecca. It is believed that it has one-fourth sanctity of Mecca. The State thus, is a favourite destination for the pilgrimage tourists.

The State is also attracting large number of tourists, specially from the foreign countries to the centre of Vaishnavaite culture propagated by Srimanta Sankardeva. The legacy of the culture has been carried still today by the *Sattras* of the State, predominantly those of Majuli.

ARCHEOLOGICAL DELIGHT

Man made attractions such as Rang Ghar, Kareng Ghar & Talatal Ghar in Sibsagar and the historical ruins of Tezpur are much archeological delights to the travellers' inquisitive minds. The Rang Ghar of Assam is a two-storied oval shaped pavilion from which Ahom royalties watched elephant fights and other sporting events. It is said to be the first ampi theatre of Asia. On the other hand there is a seven-storied palace having three underground stories—known as the Kareng Ghar built by Rudra Singha in 1699 AD. Tezpur is the place where Lord Krishna and Lord Shiva fought. Therefore, Tezpur town is also known as "City of Blood". The remains of 5th-6th century stone temples have also been discovered in the Da Parbatia area of Tezpur. Tourists from different parts of the region and country come to have a look on this man made attractions and historical ruins. There are other important archeological resources (e.g., Madan Kamdev) spread over different parts of the State

FAIRS AND FESTIVALS

Fairs and Festivals serve both as tourist attraction as well as a cause of celebration among the local populace thereby creating a sense of euphoria and brotherhood in the air. Many regular events become resources for tourism attraction. These may include competition in sport, recreation, music or the arts. From the ancient times people have moved from one place to other to attend the festivals, fairs, religious events, and exhibition, etc. The unmatched heritage of numerous races of Assam has made the State a land of festivals. The colourful festivals of the State are passionate, compelling and mesmerising. The Bihu, which is celebrated by almost all the communities of the State (albeit with different names like *Baisagu, Bisu, etc.)* are the prime festivals of the State. The two important Bihu celebrations are in January and in April. Both are celebrated on the 13-15th days of the respective months. Apart from the Bihu there are several traditional festivals celebrated with fun and gaiety, in which any tourist can take part. A few of the modern festivals are the Brahmaputra Beach Festival of Guwahati (celebrated in the month of January), Tea Festival (celebrated mainly in the month of February and March), Elephant Festival of Kaziranga National Park (January), Majuli Festival, etc. The fairs and festivals celebrated reflect the true spirit, tradition and lifestyle of Assam.

ANTHROPOLOGICAL DIVERSITY

Assam is a place of anthropological delight. It is the homeland of a rich variety of ethnic communities, the home of more than 20 ethnic subgroups. Bodo, Meches, Lalungs, Rabhas, Mishings, Karbis, Dimasas and Hajongs are some of the main tribal communities of the State. The oral traditions of different genres are rich and varied. The repertoire of traditional music, dance, and other performances of the local people are unique viewfinders to look at the mosaic of the world. These ethnic communities have got their own languages each having its own special grammar and alphabets. They have also got various cuisines, which have been the testimony of culinary arts. The handicrafts and local textiles as done by the localities are wonderful. Assam is reputed for its Silk and the most prominent variety is Muga textiles. The distinctive cultural resources of each communities of this State produce a mixture of racial, linguistic, and cultural varieties. The region is absolutely a perfect destination for tourists interested in cultures and traditions.

ADVENTURE

One of the recent trends in international tourism is traveling for active participation in adventure sports. The State of Assam has a rich potential to emerge as major adventure tourism. The land of natural richness also provides a strong ground for many adventurous activities. Tourist services like trekking, river rafting, angling, boating, fishing, mountain biking, Para sailing and swimming can be experienced in most of the tourist spots of the State. The rivers and a large number of hilly places of the State offer great opportunity for adventure sports. The rivers like Brahmaputra, Barak, and Jia-bhorali serve as important resources for the tourists interested in rafting, boating, swimming and angling. Angling in the river Jia-Bhorali is famous for Golden Mahseer fish, an endangered species. One can sport angling in Jia-bhorali with permission on a catch and release basis.

Again, rock-climbing and mountain trekking can be done in numerous hills dotting the state. The hilly terrains of the State also provide ample opportunities for mountain biking. One can view the Kaziranga, Majuli, Sibsagar, Orang National Park, Dibru-saikhowa National Park, Manas National Park, the silk weaving village of Sualkuchi by boarding the "MV Charaidew" and "MV Sukapha", the two luxury river cruises jointly operated by Assam Bengal Navigation Company (an Indo-British joint venture company) and Assam Tourism.

FEW OTHER DESTINATIONS

- *Jatinga*: A beautiful hilly place near Haflong in North Cachar district is famous for birds behaving in a mysterious way (Ornithologists try to describe this phenomenon as suicidal attempt of the birds). This strange event can be witnessed during August to November among the migratory birds. However, animal activists are against promoting Jatinga for this phenomenon. Not far away from Jatinga, the ancient ruins of the Dimasa kingdom could be found and the remains are treated with great respect due to the fact that a single piece of rock was converted into the palace of Dimasa king.
- *Sualkuchi*: It is a village situated 32 km north west of Guwahati; is one of the world's largest weaving villages often called the Manchester of the East and also known as the 'Silk town of Assam". The place is renowned as the centre of production of Assamese mulberry and Muga. The entire population here is engaged in weaving this exquisite silk fabric.
- *Digboi:* Surrounded by numerous Tea Gardens and mystic blue hills, Digboi is famous for the oldest oil refinery. The first oil refinery in Asia was established in Digboi in 1901. It is also the second one in the world. The hundred-year-old refinery and its hundred and twelve years old oil field still exist here. There is also a War Cemetery and a Golf Course in Digboi. Digboi area including Doomdooma is famous for golf courses. There are about 10 golf

courses located mostly within the compact areas of tea gardens. These offer a unique opportunity to visitors interested in golf.

- *Tezpur*: It is one of the most beautiful towns of North east India. The town is not only the centre of tourists attraction but also serves as gateways to many popular tourists destinations like Tawang, Nameri, Malinithan (archaeological site of Arunachal Pradesh), etc. The town has to offer to the visitors destinations like Agnigarh, Da Pabotia, Mahabhairab temple. Agnigarh is a beautiful tourist spot in Tezpur. According to mythology (though not supported by historical documentation), Princess Usha, the only daughter of King Bana, was kept inside the palace, which was surrounded by rampart of fire. Da Parbatia is well known for the finest and oldest specimen of sculptural or iconoclastic art in Assam. Mahabhairab temple is one of the oldest Shiva temples of Assam. The mythological belief is that King Banasura, the demon king used to worship in this Shiva temple.
- *Tea*: The tea was discovered in the wild of Assam in 1823. Since then tea has become an integral part of the Assam's economy. The tea industry of N.E. India is the one of the world's largest tea growing regions having 16 per cent share, and is the largest producer and exporter of tea in India (share 55 %). Tea Gardens are the treasure house of exotic natural beauty. Visitors from different parts enjoy the tea garden.

This is a very brief discussion on the tourism resources of Assam, and can not be claimed as exhaustive. However, these few pages are enough to establish that the State has lot to offer to the tourists and if combined with craft tourism, this place would be one of the most important attractions of the country.

REFERENCE

Bezbaruah, M. K. (1999), Tourism—Current Scenario and Future Prospects, *Yojana,* August 8, p. 7.

Sarma, M. K. (2003), Towards Positioning a Tourist Destination: A Study of North East India, *Asean Journal of Hospitality and Tourism, 2(2),* 104-117.

——, (2000), Destination positioning of north east India based on preferences and perceptions of tourists. Unpublished doctoral dissertation, Tezpur University, Tezpur.

——, (2005). Tourism Statistics for India in www.fhrai.com/mag-news/magTourismStatisticsIndia.htm browsed on 19/12/2005.

World Tourism Organisation (2004), Global troubles took toll on tourism in 2003, growth to resume in 2004, *News Releases, 27/01/2004,* Madrid. Retrieved on 22/03/2004 from http://www.world-tourism.org/Release/2003/jan/Numbers 2003.htm.

World Travel and Tourism Council (2004), *Global Travel and Tourism Poised for Robust Growth in 2004*. Retrieved on 11/03/2004 from http://www.wttc.org/News31.htm.

World Resource Institute (2003), *Tourism: International Tourism receipts*. Retrieved on 22/03/2004 from http:// earthtrends.wri.org/text/ECN/variables/252notes.htm.

World Tourism Organisation (2003). World tourism in 2002: better than expected, *News Releases, 27/01/2003*, Madrid. Retrieved on 22/03/2004 from http:// www.world-tourism.org/Release/2003/jan/Numbers2002.htm.

2

Craft and Tourism

Craftsmanship has always been a very basic activity of human society. This is because crafts and craftsmanship are integral parts of human life. In fact, they are found to be more cohesive in human relationship than even languages (Chattopadhyay, 1995), which can overcome such barriers as letters might create. This has been proved true in ancient societies in Asia, South and Central America, Africa and older countries like Greece. Crafts can exercise powerful influences and interventions on the culture of a society that are almost ageless. There are two basic objectives the crafts can fulfil. The products may help mankind in its day-to-day functions, and crafts can fulfil man's aesthetic needs. This is evident from the fact that the kings accepted mainly craft items as gifts from the neighbouring or even from a distant state. Craft can be treated as an expression of human spirit in material form, which gives delight to mankind like any so called fine arts so much so that the two may converge into one article and a fine craft in many cases can be termed an object of fine arts as well.

However, craft has another human and utilitarian angle associated with it. It is functional and helps mankind in many ways. In fact, the initial crafts were being produced to fulfil the daily needs of the human life. Basketry, pottery, bell metal works are examples of such functional use of crafts. However, in modern times many of the craft works are produced purely to fulfill aesthetic needs.

The growth of handicraft in the society is the sign of harsh hand-woven things mellowing into the fine tunes of the art and humanism. It symbolises man's endeavour to bring in elegance and rhythm to the day-to-day life, which has been full of drudgery and uncertainty. Perhaps, man's passion for creativity gave rise to songs and dances and then to crafts. From that point of view crafts are just second to songs and dance. However, as mentioned before the utilitarian approach of the craft and absence of required fine tools might have jeopardised its development into a full-fledged art form till recently.

The women folk of the ancient world took the toll of drudgery and enmity among different communities and races, and had been at the bottom of the social pyramid. However, the crafts had opened the creative vista in front of them and they too became the celebrated creators of many great craft designs and products. The textile weavers of the South and East Asian countries are the testimony of such upliftment in the social pyramid. Even today the oppressed and repressed women folk of these regions express themselves through hand woven materials, and in many cases earn for their family by selling these items in the nearby markets.

William Morris (1834-1896), proponent of famous 19th century craft revitalisation movement in Britain commented that it was necessary to reach the ideal paradise on earth and allow all people to appreciate the beauty that potentially can exist in everyday life through close interface with crafted material goods.

CRAFT AND CRAFT INDUSTRY

Craft industries can be defined as art and craft produced through skills in the use of relatively small tools without involving large economies of scale. (Markwick, 2001). De Vidas (1995) defines handicrafts as "a specific form of production and employment which creates as its product an object which represents a social group". This object provides material vehicle both for certain symbolism, and for processes of domination and manipulation.

Crafts have been perceived as authentic to the region more than anything else. It is generally believed that crafts cannot be polluted by external influences unlike other aspects of culture (i.e., dress, music, food habit, etc.). In the modern world, however, these products are integrated into circuits of production, exchange and consumption, which spread far beyond their indigenous milieu. Thus handicrafts can be seen from different perspectives: iconographic, economic, historical, technical, political, social and above all cultural. The craft of a place carries messages on the culture, economy and history of that place.

Yavary (1992) has defined handicraft as the combination of art and craft, where local raw materials are used in the process of production; the main stages of production are performed by hand with manual tools and instruments; and each product unit reflects its producer's artistic talent and mental creativity in some way. The characteristics that handicraft possesses are as follows:

1. Some main stages of production being done by hand, and others by manual tools and instruments.
2. The effective presence of human creativity in production and formation of manufactured products with diversity of designs and the techniques of carrying them out.
3. The utilisation of the main part of raw material(s) from the domestic resources.
4. Having cultural weight.
5. Dissimilarity of productive outputs with one another.
6. Not much capital investments required.
7. Having much value added.
8. Capability of being established and developed in techniques of production for generations.

The verb craft means to "make and fashion with skill" specially by hand (Hanks, 1979). These commonly include weaving, basketry, furniture, making, embroidery, jewelry, etc. Craft can also be defined as "made and designed by the same person" (Harrod, 1995). This definition encompasses fine arts within the gambit of "craft", and the boundary between these two types is hard to be erected, which might lead to slight confusion. However, a deeper analysis of this definition reveals that the craftsmen have high level of control over the whole process of designing and production. This gives a creative tag to the word. It must be remembered here that the genuine crafts are creative. However, in a later discussion we will find that all craft-works are not necessarily genuine and thus they need not be creative. Our study will, therefore, distant itself from this definition of exercising control of the design phase as this would narrow the scope of the word craft. Nevertheless, the fact remains that the crafts persons have greater control over the design of the product then their counterpart with machines. In fact a crafts person can produce a personalised or customised item without having to greatly alter the production plan.

However, it is easy to make a distinction between handmade items and machine made items, and of course the production processes which "substantially" use machine should not be treated as crafts.

According to anthropologist June Nash (1993) crafts are the medium of communication between people who *live profoundly different lives, in different countries but who can respond to the symbols, textures and forms that express a different cultural tradition.* She, in her book "Crafts in the World Market", emphasised that the industrial centres of the world are now turning back to countries which were once their colonies for seeking exotic and unique objects of handicraft production. Thus, she opines that craft production is the "weapon of the weak".

Benefits which accrue from craft and craftsmanship are manifold and this can perhaps be realised from the fact that the third world countries are earning considerable amount of export revenue by way of shipping different craft items like embroideries, jewelry and other utility items. One of the most important contributions of craft, as mentioned above, is the economic liberalisation of the weaker sections of the society, specially the women of the third world.

TOURIST SHOPPING AND CRAFTS

In the recent times shopping is regarded as one of the most "pervasive" leisure activities engaged in by the tourists (Snepenger *et al.*, 2003). Travellers from all parts of the world enjoy shopping. Even the most casual observation would indicate that shopping is the first thing tourists engage in on reaching a destination. Scholars have attached significant economic, psychological, and social implications on such shopping pursuits by the vacationers (Gunn, 1988; MacCannell, 2002 etc.). As far as economics is concerned, shopping is now the most popular activity of the tourists across the world (Snepenger *et al.*; Littrell *et al.*, 1994; Timothy *et al.*, 1995). On the other hand Kent, Shock and Snow (1983) described shopping as a pleasurable experience to millions of travellers. Timothy and Butler (1995) also have observed that shopping had been for long an important tourist activity in many destinations. These findings suggest that for many people shopping is one of the predominant activities while travelling. May be the term *suitcase tourism* aptly explicates a separate breed of tourists who travel mainly for shopping. Researches have revealed that shopping accounts for almost one-third of the total expenditure of the tourists (Godbey and Graefe, 1991; Kim and Littrell, 1999). Littrell *et al.* (1994) suggested that such shopping pursuit holds strong symbolic value as tangible evidence of the travel experience having found an "authentic" material to buy. Basically, this strongly suggests the motivation of shopping for souvenirs. Tourists use their souvenirs to think back, bolster feelings of confidence, express creativity, and enhance aesthetic pleasure (Littrell, 1990). Individuals often identify souvenirs purchased during travel as among their most prized possessions.

Much of the literature available in this context does consider handicraft as a 'tourist merchandise'. However, very few researchers (Littrell, 1990; Healy, 1994; Crippen, 2000; Revilla, Bernard and Calleja, 2000; De Vidas, 1995) documented the demand pattern of handicraft as a souvenir. Among them Revilla, Bernard and Calleja (2000) tried to profile the tourist buyers of Talavera ware-crafts (a kind of pot) in the city of Puebla in Central Mexico. On the other hand, Littrell (1990) studied the tourists' attitude towards hand woven textile and developed profiles of international tourist buyers. Healy (1994) dealt with handicraft very briefly in his study on tourist merchandise. He basically studied the motivating factors for souvenir purchase. De Vidas (1995) took up the textile of Andes as the theme of his study. Crippen too studied the textile craft of Batik or *ikat* of Indonesia. It is observed that all these studies looked at only one kind of craft at a time.

Craft can be used in the present day for nostalgia, particularly a sense of "longing" for the 'good old days' beyond industrialisation and urbanisation (Creighton, 2001).

Although traditionally the crafts have been produced for local use in daily life, increasingly it is seen that mostly they are being produced to suit an external market. An external market is a cluster of consumers, which are not from the craft-producing region. As a necessary corollary, the external market would constitute mostly of tourists. There has been extensive discussion concerning use of crafts in relation to tourism. There exists a steady demand of craft products among tourists, so much so that some tourists would visit a destination only to experience the making of crafts and buy them as souvenirs of their visit. When a tourist chooses to buy a craft item she is buying (knowingly or unknowingly) a message to be taken home. Tourists help in many ways in preserving the heritage and culture of the host country. Many examples can be drawn from around the world on how the industry is really contributing local culture in surviving the stiff and ruthless competition of time and globalisation. Inflow of tourists helps in establishment of 'indigenous entrepreneurs' in the vicinity of the attractions. This facilitates selling of merchandise specifically produced by local artisans as souvenirs to the tourists. Many destinations in India are full of such merchandise sellers and the business generated by this is tremendous. Many researchers (De Vidas, 1995; Porananond, 2000) have dealt with this issue of local entrepreneurs near the tourist places. Where crafts are solely produced for tourists the craft is sometimes named as "tourist craft" in tourism literature.

Craft industry constitutes most of the village and cottage industry, which are operating on a very tiny level, and mostly as a secondary employment of the producers. Economies of the third world countries are highly dependent on such cottage level industries. However, it is observed that craft industries have become more commercialised in the recent years and are thus producing more efficiently than ever before. Many such industries have undergone changes in the product, the production process and in product features. This is mainly due to the influence of the external market, and the products are suited to the demand pattern of the mass buyers. As the same products are mass-produced some amount of machinery intervention is also necessary for the basic shape of the craft work. However, such transformation will definitely erode the "authenticity" and certain "exoticeness" of the product will be vanishing. There has been a long-standing debate as to whether the crafts be allowed to undergo changes.

AUTHENTICITY

According to Sapir (1924) authenticity is "*persons, intimate cluster of persons, communities or societies, whose lived experience is harmonious with, or true to, their inherent or intrinsic cultural structure or historically emergent form*". Thus authenticity is a historically emergent form of anything that can be attributed to a group of people, for example, a community. Authenticity is a holistic term that emphasises the existence of a flow of collective knowledge or process that arises from the "lived experience" of the members of the community. Therefore, anything that's indigenous to the group of people (that's being referred to) is authentic. The customs, beliefs, dress, food, rituals, festivals which have the historical touch (or flow) are authentic. Authenticity, from the perspective of tourism can be defined as "*a desired experience and benefit associated with the visit to certain types of tourism destination. It is presumed to be the result of an encounter with true, uncommecialised, everyday life in a culture different than that of the tourist*" (Smith, 1990).

A noted theorist Cohen (1988) argues that authenticity is not a 'primitive given', which cannot change over time. But, it is 'negotiable'. This is also supported by other theorists who suggest that culture is a dynamic process, and anything that is attached to that culture is bound to change. Some tourists often seek to move from 'front stage' to 'back stage' in their quest for knowing the unknown, away from the superficial world of pleasure tourism in an intimate experience (Goffman, 1959). As Littrell *et al.* had pointed out in 1993, in such searches for authenticity tourists look for signs of originality and uniqueness as prominent criteria. Littrell *et al.* (1994) have also pointed out that authenticity includes a craft's historical integrity and genuineness. Traditional practices that have marked associations with a place or people in that place can also be treated as authentic. An authentic item should give an impression of a 'state of non-ordinary'. Shenhav-Keller (1995) in her study of Israeli souvenir trade concluded that authenticity might be determined by the following five dimensions:

1. Hand-craftsmanship,
2. Art and aesthetic,
3. Local originality,
4. Cultural roots and historical past, and
5. Ritual objects.

Culture, as such is intangible. However, characteristics that define culture are usually expressed in cultural heritage and cultural societies (Robinson as cited by Carter, 2004). These are the material manifestation of culture and can be seen in cultural expressions, traditions and resources (Carter, 2004). For a tourist the cultural materialism might be the exposure to different customs, rituals expressed in terms of dances, songs and other staged activities. But such authentic experiences except for some objects must be consumed on site. As MacCannell (1976) observed, search of authenticity has been a major driving force for the tourists as they are often in the look out for an "object" that could be carried off-site. Appadurai (1986) has suggested that authentic objects are made by the people they represent and nothing can, therefore, be more authentic than a hand-made item. Nothing perhaps, can exhibit the tourists' visit to the destination better than a hand-made product, which can be safely termed as authentic.

Therefore, the possession of a hand-made item may symbolise attachment with the host society. And tourists are in the look out of an authentic item to buy as a souvenir. This may be one of the vital reasons why handicrafts have been the objects of desire for the travellers. Authenticity with respect to culture is associated with the motif, colour, design and most importantly the use (utility) of the craft at the host region. The item will be more authentic if the craft is unique in these aspects and can easily be identified with the host populace.

Craft-works are widely believed to be authentic by the tourists. Therefore, those who are looking for authenticity in souvenir purchases would definitely look for some crafts of the region. Blundell (1993) reported that westerners trust a product as authentic if only the products made by the people who are represented by these products. Thus handicrafts possess a very good chance to be treated as authentic among the tourists.

COMMODIFICATION OF CRAFT

Crafts-works now-a-days have undergone tremendous changes. These changes are mainly manifested by the alteration in the use of craft products. Crafts around the world are no longer produced only for utilitarian purposes. There was an era when the self-sufficient villagers of a remote corner of the world would have used their skill in craft making for producing objects of daily use by employing simple tools like a small knife or a wheel. Gifted craftsman would have produced whatever was necessary within the household and pass on a few spare ones to those who might be in need. People were happy and self-content during that time. Slowly barter system came to existence and craft products started to be bartered in local *hat* or village festivals. Probably that was the time people began to realise the economic importance of craft products. And special communities took over the responsibilities of producing a unique craft. For example, in Assam, *kamar*s are traditionally producing earthen pots while the *kamar*s are skilled at iron weapon crafting. The economic importance of craft products got a tremendous boost as the barter system was replaced by exchange. Scrupulous and pure craftsmen then started to produce the crafts in large quantity so that they could earn a livelihood. Even then few crafts, specially in Assam were produced by almost all village households. This tradition can even now been seen in some villages in Assam. Textile and bamboo products are even today being crafted in almost all households in the villages in Assam. A discussion on such crafts and its transformation is offered later in this report.

As the utilitarian handicrafts are replaced by the more efficient and cheap products produced by machines, the demand for craft to be used in mankind's day-to-day life has suffered a reverse. The economic impact of this on the artisans is devastating. This may in the long run totally imbalance the craft industry and like in many countries, this beautiful form of art is going to survive only on Government sponsorship. Tourism is one such intervention that helps in recreating the values of the tradition through handicrafts and handlooms that had been lost in the materialistic world.

The moment the "utilitarian" tag went off the craft products, the craftsmen, and the communities who lived on crafts making started to look for some avenues of mass production of the materials so that the aggression of cheap and more durable products made by modern day machine aluminum, steel and plastic can be tackled. Many did not succeed in the process and bowed away to another trade. Such traditional artisan families have since been shifted to other beneficial trades to earn their livelihood. This had threatened to create socio-economic inter-sector migration. Those who survived learned many lessons, and one of them is to become more professional in the sense that crafts could be produced and sold in a commercial way. And "commercialisation of crafts" began.

Crafts can be commercialised under widely different historical perspectives (Cohen 1988). '*Spontaneous commercialisation*' is a process that sees the changes occur gradually through growing contacts with outsiders like tourists. This is a natural process and the products that go through this process may not be termed as un-authentic as such. However, this may not be as smooth a transition as the nature itself. For example, during the time of Industrial revolution the hand made items rapidly gave way to the machine-made items. This, at that point of time, was commercialisation. But now the same products can be treated as authentic to those ages. Sometimes commercialisation happens more rapidly due to certain sudden changes, development or historical intervention when the craftsmen use local skills to meet outside demands. This may not be necessarily related to the producer's culture. This is known as '*sponsored commercialisation*'. For example, Malta and Thailand are not traditionally known for glass blowing craft. However, the demand for such work among the tourists had led to growth of such industries in those regions. And tourists generally flock on the craft villages producing such items. It is interesting to note that the mass of tourists are more attracted towards the exotic craft rather than the traditional or 'authentic' ones. Therefore, it may not be totally wrong to start a new craft altogether just to satisfy the external demand.

Sponsored innovative commercialisation is another form of commercialisation of crafts where an outside agency sponsors the whole process of commercialisation. As it is evident from the term the outsiders are least interested in preserving the local stylistic elements, and thus encourage growing heterogeneisation. The capitalist "globalised village" may be one of the main reasons for such commercialisation. Other forms of craft commercialisation are *complementary commercialisation* and *substitutive commercialisation.* As the terms suggest the former one is complementary to an existing craft form while the latter one is a substitute of such craft.

REFERENCE

Blundell, V. (1993), Aboriginal empowerment and souvenir trade in Canada, *Annals of Tourism Research, 20(1)*, 64-87.

Carter, B. W. (2004), Tourists as cultural groups. *Tourist Behaviour*, ed. A Raj. New Delhi: Kanishka.

Cohen, E. (1988), Authenticity and commoditisation of tourism, *Annals of Tourism Research of Tourism Research, 15*(3), 371-386.

Creighton, M. (2001), Spinning silk, weaving selves: Nostalgia, gender and identity in Japanese craft vacations, *Japanese Studies, 21(1)*, 5-29.

Crippen, Kaye (2000), The threads that tie textiles to tourism. In M. Hitchcock and W. Nuryanti, Eds. *Building on Batik. The Globalization of a Craft Community*, Hants: Ashget Publishing Limited.

De Vidas, Anath Ariel (1995), Textiles, memory and the souvenir industry in the Andes in M. F. Lanfant, John B. Allcock and Edward M. Bruner, eds., *International Tourism, Identity and Change*, London, Sage Publication.

Godbey, G. and Graefe, A. (1991), Repeat tourism, play and monetary spending, *Annals of Tourism Research, 18(2)*, 213-225.

Goffman, E. (1959), The Presentation of Self in Everyday Life., New York: Doubleday.

Gunn, C. (1988). *Vacation Scape*, New York: Van Nostrand Brindhole Company.

Hanks, P. (Ed.) (1979), *Collins Dictionary of English Language*, London, Collins.

Harrod, T. (1995), *The Crafts in Britain in the 20th Century*, New Haven, CT, Yale University Press.

Healy, Robert G. (1994), 'Tourist merchandise' as a means of generating local benefits from tourism, *Journal of Sustainable Tourism, 2(3)*, 137-151.

Kim, S. and Littrell, M. (1999), Predicting souvenir purchase intentions. *Journal of Travel Research, 38(2)*, 153-162.

Littrell, L. (1990), Symbolic significance of textile crafts for tourists, *Annals of Tourism Research, 17(2)*, 228-245.

Littrell, Mary Ann, Baizerman, Suzane, Kean Rita, Gahring, S.,

Niemeyer, S, Reilly, Rae and Stout, JaneAnn (1994), Souvenirs and tourism styles. *Journal of Travel Research 33(1)*, 3-11.

MacCannell, D. (1976), Staged authenticity: Arrangements of social space in tourist settings, *American Journal of Sociology, 79(3)*, 589-603.

Porananond, P. (2000), Tourism and cultural changes: the crafts of Chiang Mai in M. Robinson, N. Evans, P. Long, R. Sharply and J. Swarbrooke, eds., *Reflections on International Tourism. Expressions of Culture, Identity and Meaning in Tourism*, Sunderland, Business Education Publishers Ltd.

Sapir, E. (1924), Culture, genuine and spurious, *American Journal of Sociology, 29*, 401-429.

Shenhav-Keller, Shelly (1995), The Jewish pilgrim and the purchase of souvenir in Israel in M. F. Lanfant, John B. Allcock and Edward B. Bruner, eds., *International Tourism, Identity and Change*. London: Sage Publication.

Smith, S. (1990), Dictionary and Concepts in Recreation and Leisure Studies, Westport, CT, Greenwood Publishing Group.

Snepenger, D. J., Murphy, Leann, O'Connell, Ryan and Gregg, Eric (2003), Tourists and residents use of a shopping space. *Annals of Tourism Research, 30(3)*, 567-580.

Timothy, Dallen J., Butler and Richard, W. (1995), Cross border shopping: a North American perspective, *Annals of Tourism Research, 22(1)*, 16-34.

Yavary, H. (1992), A glance at Iranian handicrafts. *Hands and Creativity*, published by Iran Handicrafts Organisation, Spring 1992 in http://www.irvl.net/IRAN42.HTM, retrieved on 20/03/2004

3

Major Tribes of Assam

Any discussion on traditional craft of a region cannot be completed without throwing some lights on the tribal culture of that area, as the tribes are the originator of any creative works like craft. The magical touch of the craft workers and their creations form important part of the heritage of a tribe. Hence a very brief discussion is offered below on some major tribes that has been dotting the cultural orchestra of the state of Assam.

THE BODOS

Bodo, a community of the Kachari, constitute the largest group among the tribal populations of Assam. They are distributed all over Assam, but their major concentration is in the Kokrajhar, Darrang, Kamrup and Goalpara districts. The Bodos are now at home in the newly formed Bodoland Territorial Council (BTC) consisting of the districts mentioned above with some newly carved districts. Topographically, the concentration is seen in the foothills of Bhutan across the international boarder (Kokrajhar in the west and Sonitpur in the East). According to the 1991 census their population was 12,67,015 (44.08% of total Scheduled Tribes population in Assam). According to some scholars the Bodos were the first agricultural nomads who have entered Assam and introduced agriculture and irrigation. Besides, it is believed that the Bodos introduced sericulture in Assam.

The Bodo village is a self-sufficient unit. It is said that India has received the technique of weaving and embroidery from Indo-Mongoloids. In Assam, the Bodos were decidedly the pioneers in this respect. The domestic animals of the Bodos are principally confined to common cattle and pigs. A Bodo thatched house in the village is seldom distinguishable from the so-called "Assamese" houses in structure and architecture. The house is usually a two-roof affair erected on the ground with scanty ventilation. The family looms are generally placed on the backyard. Agriculture is the main occupation of the Bodos. The Bodo women rear different kinds of silkworms including the mulberry and Erhee. The Bodo women look distinctive in their traditional attire, the *dokhana, Arnai* and blouse.

Bodos have a very powerful language of their own. The Bodo language in the course of time spread over a large area right from Sadiya in eastern Assam to Tripura. Bodos living basically in the foothills of Bhutan have traditionally distinct dresses for women from those who reside elsewhere. Women of the former group wear only one unsewn piece wrapped in more than one fold through the whole length of the body, while the later wear a *Dokhna* encircling the body from the breast-line down to a little above the heels. Married women add another piece to cover upper portion. However these distinctions are no longer seen in the urban areas. The two pieces of prominent textiles *Riha* and

Mekhala worn by socalled Assamese women is believed to be improvised form of the original dress of the Bodo women.

The Bodo society has been divided into certain groups (as in the case of other civilised societies in India) based mainly on the principle of labour such as like the *Basumatari* (land owners), *Gayari* (in charge of arcanut cultivation), *Tamular* (in charge of betel-leaf cultivation), *Musahari, Narjary, Sargawari, Sibirgri, Doimari, Gaya* and *Brahmari*. However, They no longer perform these roles. The social structure of the Bodos is primarily patriarchal. The father is the head of the family. The tribe generally practices marriage by negotiation. A Bodo youth can earn a bride by serving in her family. The Bodos generally follow exogamy. Residence after marriage is patrilocal and both inheritance and succession are through the eldest son. Women play significant roles in agriculture, fishing, animal husbandry, collection of fuel and other economic activities. The dead are cremated or buried. After ten days, the *daha*, a post-funeral ceremony is performed.

The Bodos are known for agriculture and they go for improved agriculture with irrigated lands. Natural resources are controlled by individual proprietors and also by the village headman with the help of village elders. They are well known in the art of preserving paddy seeds and digging indigenous canal system to irrigate their fields. Their production of food obviously depends on their dietary habits. Rice is the staple food like other non-tribal neighbours. Some percentage of rice is also used in brewing rice beer called "Jumai" which is cherished by most Bodos except those who believe in the Brahmanism. The members of the community also relish the dehydrated powder of the Sun-dried fishes called *Nakam* and almost all the households preserve quite a large amount of *Nakam* for use during monsoon. The art of fishing and hunting and preserving dehydrated meat and fish are part of Bodo culture. They also cultivate pumpkin, arecanut, cucumber, brinjals, potato, etc. for their need. Some members of the community are engaged in business and government and private services. Sericulture and weaving play important roles in their economy. The function of their traditional village council is limited to settle disputes.

Traditionally the Bodos had their own religion, which later was influenced by Hinduism, first by the Shakta cult and later by the Vaisnavite cult of Srimanta Sankardeva. They believed in a supreme deity of *Bathou* and His consort *Mainao*. It is believed that propitiation of *Bathou* and *Mainao* in the month of October and November (*Aswin* and *Kati* months) gives abundant yield of crops. Later with the influence of Hinduism *Bathou* and *Mainao* was equated with Lord Shiva and his consort Parvati or Durga. A part of Bodos had a change in faith later, who are known as *Brahmas*. The *Brahmas* are the followers of Kalicharan Brahma. The traditional Bodo also believes in a number of spirits and Gods in addition to their supreme Gods *Bathou* and *Mainao*. Some Bodos also believe in Hindu deities like *Laxmi, Kamakhya, Biswakarma*, etc.

The traditional creativity of the Bodos is recognised all over Assam, and in the entire North Eastern India. The

Bodos rear the Erhee cocoons, spin and weave quality warm cloth. The usual feed plant for Erhee silk worm is Bhotera, which the Bodos plant as hedge. The Bodos of Kokrajhar-belt rear a type of Erhee cocoon which is red in colour and which is believed to be endemic to that area. They are used to spin the cocoons with the help of their wooden spinner but as it stands now they are switching over to paddle operated spinning machine, which is known as "Chowdhuri Charkha" named after its inventor. The Bodos of central and upper Assam also rear the Muga and Mulberry silk cocoons. Both men and women, wear a scarf called *patani*, which has diverse geometrical forms on the borders in an ensemble of branching floral stems, sometimes with butterflies between them. Their fabrics have charming designs such as men on horses, floral and mango patterns, birds and diamond shapes. The Bodo men are famous for their cane and bamboo works producing mind-boggling baskets and, of late, furniture too. There are also good Bodo potters, blacksmiths, goldsmiths and carpenters who meet their indigenous demand. In brief this productivity is a part of Bodo cultural heritage.

The contribution of the Bodos to the musical mosaic of Assam is very significant. The traditional Bodos have their festivals and ceremonies. *Kherai* is their principal festival celebrated during October and November. This is the festival when the Bodos pray to their supreme deities *Bathou* and *Mainao* by way of Puja similar to the Hindus by making sacrifices. The *Domangshi* or the *Baisagu* festival is another occasion of much merry making. In the *Baisagu* dance, which is part of the festival, participated by everyone irrespective of age and sex. The *Bagurumba* dance where only the girls and women participate is instituted at the time of paddy plantation. In fact the dances are part and parcel of Bodo culture. The Bodo dance *Doudini Mochanai* is believed to have given rise to *Deodhini Nritya* prevalent in Assam. Bodo musical instruments like *Sifung* also called *Swifin* (flute), *Kham* (the great drum), *Jotha* (cymbal), *serja* (violin type) and *Dhontra* (guiter of two strings) have enriched the music and dance of Assam. According to some scholars, Assamese *Bihu* and *Bhatheli* festival had their origins in the Bodo spring festival.

THE MISHINGS

The Mishings are also known as "Miri" in the colloquial terms. But for the Mishings, Miri is one who performs the role of the priest. They prefer to call themselves Mishing, meaning a noble person. Once the Mishing were the inhabitants of the hilly areas of East Siang and Lower Subansiri districts of Arunachal Pradesh. The folk literature of the people shows that they migrated down to the Brahmaputra valley years before the advent of the Ahoms in Assam. The Mishings are distributed in the plains of North Lakhimpur, Jorhat, Dibrugarh, Sibsagar and Darrang districts of Assam and in the East Siang District of Arunachal Pradesh. According to the 1991 census their population was 4,67,790 (16.27% of total Scheduled Tribes population). They speak their own dialect, a Tibeto-Burman language. It is their mother tongue and they are also conversant with Assamese and Hindi. They use the Assamese and *Devanagiri* scripts.

The Mishing people usually live near the riverbanks with raised platform made of bamboo. A Mishing village usually consists of 50 or more houses built generally on two sides of a barren. They rear cattle and pigs in an extensive manner. Traces of primitive socialism still exist amongst the Mishings. They have *Pigbo* and *Daglik* system, where the village community extends help in the shape of personal labour to individual houses at the time of need. In most villages all the villagers share individual hunt however small the game may be. Their production of crops depends completely upon on monsoon. Rice is the staple food of the Mishing. It is their tradition that they brew rice beer called "Apong", which is cherished by most Mishings and used in their traditional works called "Uie". Like the Bodos Mishings too relish the dehydrated powder of the dried fishes called "Namsing" and almost all the households preserve quite a large amount of "Namsing" for future use. The art of fishing and preserving dehydrated meat and fish are part of Mishing culture like that of most of the tribes of Assam.

The Mishings of Assam are divided into several exogamous clans. Cross-cousin marriage is prevalent, and monogamy is the usual form of their marriage. Incidences of inter-caste marriage with neighbouring communities have been seen as the result of modern thoughts and approaches. "Dugla Yamne Lanam" meaning marriage by elopement is one of the chief forms of marriage sanctioned by the Mishing society. Newly married couples usually start an independent household. The women enjoy considerable rights in social and economic spheres but they do not participate in political activities (Map 1).

Cultivation and fishing are their major occupations, and they supplement their income by working as agricultural labourers. They also generate income by rearing cattle, pigs, hens, ducks, pigeons, etc. Particularly the young girls of the family take major responsibility in this occupation. The Mishing women rear all kinds of silkworms, spin and weave the quality cloth for their own use. They use to spin the cocoons with the help of wooden spinner. Mishing women are expert weavers. They weave their own cloth particularly the colourful scarves. They put on scarves made of Erhee fabric, which are often designed with human figures, flower, butterflies and geometric patterns. Colour and designs play important parts in these fabrics. Impressions of horses, elephants, butterflies, peacocks, tigers, fish, dolls and legendary figures are frequently used as designs in their textiles. Apart from scarves they make draperies, headgears and bags with these designs.

The Mishing men are famous for their cane and bamboo works. They produce their household items like-baskets, nets, pots, mats, etc. The headman (*Gaon Burah*), who is elected to the post, administers a Mishing village. The Mishings believe in the existence of spirits or supernatural beings called "Uie", which are hostile to men. It is believed that *Uie* are responsible for diseases, sickness, death and destruction. The mountains, streams, rivers, forest, moon, sun, and ponds according to them, are the abodes of these

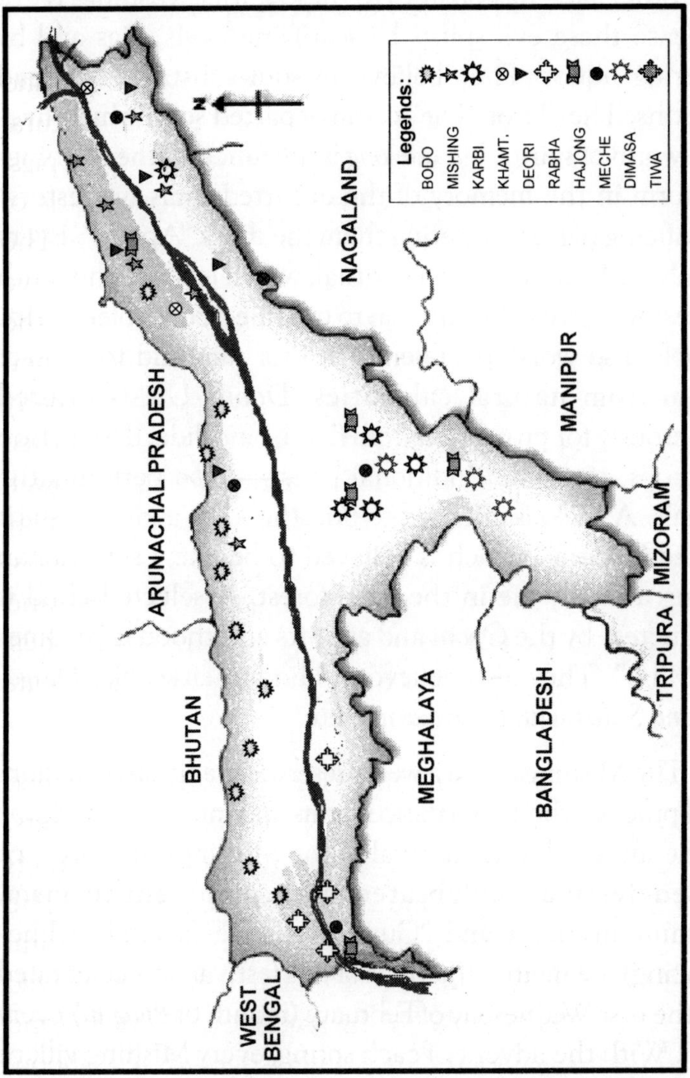

Map 1: Assam Concentration of Tribes

sprits. They attributed illness, accident, unnatural death and other such misfortunes to these spirits. Mishings try to appease these evil spirits by scarifying fowls, pigs and by offering liquor. They believe in soul-substance of dead persons. The "Urom Uie" is the departed soul, which lives in a world of spirits. *Uie aamong* is the function the Mishings perform in the memory of the departed souls (ancestors) sacrificing pigs and offering them the drink "Apong". Every family performs *Urom aapin* ritual, which lets free the ninth ancestor to live in *Sumin-Soin* to become a benevolent deity. People also worship "Taleng Uie" for rain and to protect them from natural calamities. *Dobur Uie* is offered generously for protection from flood, landslide, destruction of crops, etc. The traditional priest—*Mibo* performs the rituals. A *Mibo* is initiated to priesthood by a kind of spirit called "Opom", which is believed to be like a sub-human living a family life in the deep forest. A selected child is 'abducted' by the *Opom* and after its adulthood it becomes a "Mibo". They also believe in Hindu deities like *Durga, Laxmi, Saraswati, Biswakarma*, etc.

The Mishings have a well-preserved tradition of folklore and practice their own dance forms and music. *Ali-ai-ligang* is the most colourful festival of the Mishings. It is an agri-based festival, celebrated with great enthusiasm. Community feast and "Gumrag" dance (a kind of line-dancing) are main attractions of this festival. It is celebrated on the first Wednesday of February (month of *Phagun*) every year. With the advent of each spring, every Mishing village is plunged into gay euphoria. When they get an exceptionally good harvest they celebrate *Narasingha Bihu*.

Their most popular form of songs among them are called "Oinitom", with a very melodious and heart rendering tune. Many *Bihu* tunes of modern Assamese language are borrowed from this indigenous form of music. They observe a ceremony known as *Payday* for the well being of the newborn. The dead is buried outside the village boundary and the mourning period continues for five days. On the 10th or 12th day, community feasts are arranged.

THE KARBIS

Karbis are one of the oldest tribes residing in Assam. In earlier days they were also known as Mikir. Now they prefer to call themselves *Arleng*, meaning man or Karbi. According to the Karbi myth, their forefathers came from Knong Piller, a mountain, somewhere near the northeastern border. Karbis first inhabited a mountain somewhere between Diphu (now the headquarters of the Karbi Anglong Autonomous Council) and Dimapur (a busy business town of Nagaland adjacent to Assam border). At the present times a majority of them dwell in the Karbi-Anglong district and some pockets of the adjoining North Cachar Hills, Sibsagar, Nagaon and Darrang districts of Assam. The process of convergence of the Karbis into the broader so-called Assamese society began only during the Ahom rule. In Assam their population, according to the 1991 census, was 2,85,811 (9.94% of total tribal population). The Karbi language, which belongs to the Bodo group of the Tibeto-Burman family of languages, is their mother tongue. The Roman script is used. They exhibit Mongoloid features.

These people differ from the Bodo group. They are non-vegetarians but avoid eating beef. Rice is their staple food. Homemade rice beer (*har*) is their favourite beverage.

The Karbis are divided into four broad social groups, namely *Chinthong, Ronghang, Amra and Dumrali.* These groups are again divided into various exogamous clans (*lon* or *kur*) like *Ingty, Inghy, Tehran, Timang* and *Terang* and sub-clans or surnames like *Timung, Terron,* etc. Karbis are very strict about the sanctity of marriage. Marriage beyond the community was not preferred, but such marriage is now socially approved. Monogamy is the common form. Though polygamy is permissible, cases of such marriages are very rare. Adult marriage is commonly practiced and mates are generally acquired through negotiation, service and elopement. Boys and girls are allowed to meet at *Chamangkan* (a festival) when they dance together. Most of the Karbi families are nuclear and they trace descent through the male line. The property is handed down from father to son; succession goes to the eldest son. The women participate in agricultural operations and look after the household jobs. They are not allowed to participate in religious functions. Birth is considered to be the return of a soul to the world of the living. A woman has to observe various kinds of restrictions when she conceives a child. When a death occurs, relatives from even a distant place pay a visit. The dead is cremated and afterwards a death ceremony called *ehomangkon* is performed for three to four days.

In Meghalaya, the Karbis are notified as *Mikir* and they

are concentrated in the Jaintia and East Khasi Hills districts bordering the Karbi Anglong district of Assam. Rice is their staple cereal that is eaten with pulses and vegetables. Their home-brewed rice beer is known as *horlong*. Men are habitual smokers. Milk is a new addition to their diet. These people are divided into five clans called *Kur*, which are *Terang, Teron, Enghee, Engti* and *Timung*.

The *Mikirs* of Arunachal Pradesh are now known as Karbi. Their earlier name was *Arleng*. They migrated to their present habitat in recent years. They live in the Balijan circle of the Lower Subansiri district of Arunachal Pradesh. With others they use Assamese, Hindi and English and the scripts used for communicating with others are Assamese, *Devanagari* and Roman. Basketry is their only craft, and they make baskets for domestic use only.

THE KHAMTIS

The Khamtis are believed to be a section of the Thai. Their original habitat was reported to be from *Mung Khamti Long* or *Boor Khamti* or *Manshi* in Upper Myanmar. The migration occurred in the early part of the eighteenth century. At the present day Khamtis are found in Bihpuria and Narayanpur areas of Lakhimpur district and in Sadia region of upper Assam. They speak Khamti-Shan. The division of the community of the Khamtis are—*Bor-Khamti, Moonglair-Khamti, Kmajangs, Phakials, Shan* and *Aitonia*. The Khamti belong to the Mongoloid stock and are characterised by a short stature, a bigger head and a flat nose. Rice is their staple food, and they relish fish, fowl, pig, goat, wild bear and deer.

They construct their residences on raised platforms of 4 feet to 5 feet above the ground level. The roof is made of leaves found abundantly in the jungles of the area (Takou or Jengu leaves). Every household has at least two or three fireplaces. Almost all households possess a granary or a cowshed-cum granary. Weaving is performed in the space between the ground and the elevated floor of the main house. Weaving in the family loom is not only favourite pastimes for the ladies, but also an important cottage industry for them. Most of the domestic requirements of cloths especially for the womenfolk are met from the family loom. They rear pigs and fowls in abundance. In the field men are assisted by their wives. They have apt hands for embroidery and amuse themselves by manufacturing silver pipes, brass bowls and other small crafts of the same kind, which are neatly made.

Originally every village had two separate dormitories, one for the unmarried boys and the other for the unmarried girls. But nowadays this dormitory system is not found in many villages.

Traditionally the Khamtis are cultivators, businessmen and timber merchants. The Khamtis are an economically stratified community. Cooperation in the agricultural activities is also a salient feature of the Khamti society. They practice permanent wet rice cultivation. The poor can live peacefully on the benign protection of the rich. A hereditary village chief, the *Chow-fa*, who is assisted by the *How-sing* and *Chowoog Mung*, heads their traditional village council, the *Mug Chum*. In a Khamti village there may be a hereditary King, who is respected even today by all the villagers. Next in the social hierarchy is the *Keman* or *Gaonbura* who has to perform his duties in consultation with the King. After the *Gaonbura* the next position of honour goes to the *Pathak*, who acts as a guide in all the religious activities.

Marriage in the same clan is prohibited, but there may be a few cases of endogamous marriage. The Khamtis are monogamous. There are mainly two types of marriages among the Khamtis, viz., formal and informal. In the formal type guardians of the prospective boy and girl take the initiative. The commonest type of marriage is the informal one. Marriage between a King's clan and an ordinary clan is not forbidden.

The Khamtis are Hinajan Buddhists. At least in religious matters the Khamtis even today try to keep close contact with the Burmese. On the basis of religion the people in a village can be divided into two broad divisions, viz., those elderly people who follow the eight principles of Buddhism (Asstasheel) and those who follow the five principles of Buddhisn (Panchasheel). The Khamti festivals are very closely connected with their religious beliefs. *Poi Changken* or *Pani Bihu* is held every year in the month of April. Generally, it synchronizes with the Assamese *Rongali Bihu*. The next important festival is *Poi Nen Hok*, i.e., Buddha *purnima* held in the month of May. Prayers to Lord Buddha and offering of gifts to the monks are the highlights of the festival. *Paribot* or *Paribasa* is a religious festival meant only for the monks. It is a ceremony for self-purification of the monks. The Khamtis practice both cremation and burial of their death. The death ceremony is observed on the sixth day. Entertaining the villagers with a big feast and offering of gifts to the monks form the nucleus of the ceremony.

THE DEORIS

The Deories are a priestly section of the Chutiya community of Assam. According to the 1991 census their population was 35,849 (1.25% of the total tribal population). They are predominately rural. They are divided into four territorial groups, namely *Dobongya*, *Tengapniya*, *Borgonya* and *Patorgonya*. According to some scholars-the name Deori has originated from the word devgrihika, meaning a priest or one in charge of the temple. During the rein of the Ahom King, Swargadeu Gaurinath Singha, Deories had migrated from the Lohit district of Arunachal Pradesh. Nowadays, the population of the Deories stretches up to parts of Lakhimpur, Dibrugarh, Sibsagar, Jorhat and Sonitpur districts. Their mother tongue is Deori, which belongs to the Bodo group of the Tibeto-Burman family of languages. But they use the Assamese language and script for inter-community communication.

The Deories are divided into a number of clans. They are *Sundhariya*, *Patriya*, *Dupiya*, *Marangaya*, *Chariya*, *Lagasuya*, *Chitigaya*, *Mehedaya*, *Kuliya*, *Airiya*, *Kumataya*,

Bihiya, Khutiya, Machiya, etc. The existence of two subdivisions in the Dibongya group has also been reported. The Deories are generally monogamous and often marriage precedes courtship and elopement. The system of paying bride price is prevented among them. A Deori wife lives at her husband's place, most of whom live in joint families. Parental property is inherited equally by the sons. They perform *mimo hareruba* to propitiate the deceased ancestors by offering sacrifices.

The economy of the Deori centers on agriculture. The traditional Deori headman is known as *Gaonbura* and the community council is called *Mel*. Rice is the staple food of the Deori and they regularly drink rice beer called *Sujen*. In a few villages the Deories observe their traditional tribal festivals. Their chief deity is *Gira Girach*; *Picha Dema. Pichachi and Demachi* are the two other important deities. They celebrate the festivals, *Bohagiyo* and *Maghiyo Bisu* with great enthusiasm. Owing to their close interaction with a number of neighbouring Hindu communities a few Hindu rituals are also practiced by them. Traditional relations like *suriya mata* and *hareruba* act as a cementing factor and help the growth of fellow felling and integration among the members of the community.

THE RABHAS

Rabha habitats are mainly spread over the lower Assam districts of Goalpara, Dhubri and Kokrajhar. Rabhas are also dwelling in Garo hills of Meghalaya and in the north

West Bengal. Linguistically, Rabha belongs to the Bodo group of the Tibeto-Burman family of languages. Most of the Rabhas are well conversant with Assamese and Bengali. They generally use the Assaamese script. There are four distinct groups among them, namely *Rongdani, Maitori, Pati and Dhuri*. These can be described as dialect groups.

The Rabhas are non-vegetarians. Rice is their staple cereal. Rice beer, locally known as *Choko*, is their favourite drink, and it is served on almost all religious, social and festive occasions. The Rabha have a number of clans (*bari*), such as *Hato, Tara*, *Bantho* and *Dipha* some of which bear names of plants, animals, fish, hill or rivers. The dialectal differences between the *Rongdani* and *Maitori* are little and inter-marriages between these two groups take place freely. Monogamy is the norm. Adult marriage is preferred. Post-marriage residence is patrilocal. Marriage through negotiation is in practice among the *Rongdani* and *Maitori* Rabha. The *Pati* and *Dhuri* groups have largely adopted the marriage pattern of their neighbouring Hindu communities. The marriage ceremony generally takes place at the bridegroom's residence with the sacrifices of a pair of chickens to the family deity. Their priest (*Deori*) conducts the marriage proceedings. Of late, many families of the *Pati* section engage Brahmin priests to perform marriage rites. Divorce and the remarriage of divorcees, widows and widowers are allowed.

The Rabhas have retained the matrilineal line of descent to some extent, but not matrilineal inheritance. The position of authority in the family is inherited by the eldest son. In the rural areas the Rabha women do the entire household work and participate in agricultural operations also. The Rabha cremate the dead. The *Rongdani* traditionally do not perform any post-death rites. The *Maitori* observe mourning for fifteen days, and during this period they adhere to vegetarian diet. The *Pati* and *Dhuri* sections have largely adopted the Assamese Hindu ways of performing rites and rituals connected with death.

Agriculture is the principal economic pursuit of the Rabhas. The Rabha practices both wet and dry cultivation and grow paddy, jute, mustard, pulses and sugarcane. Fishing is their subsidiary occupation.

The traditional mechanism of social control of the Rabhas functions through a three-tier system. There is a council at the village level, which deals with social disputes and offences of a minor nature.

The Rabha believes that all ailments and sufferings are caused by the evil influence of some deities and such deities should be propitiated to get rid of maladies. In the religious practices, there is a great variation as regards the absorption of Hindu elements, by different sections of the Rabhas. The principal religious festivals of the Rabhas are related to *Khokshi Bai* or *Bai-Kho* (goddess of the crop), and Hachong (village deity). During *Bai-Kho* the youth sing *Sathar* songs to the accompaniment of *Kara* flute and *Singa*. The Rabha women are experts at weaving, which they do to meet their household needs. The Rabhas are rich in folk-song and folk-dances. Kingfisher is the sacred bird of the Rabhas.

THE HAJONGS

The Hajongs are one of the numerically small tribal communities of Assam. They are Scheduled as a tribe in the two autonomous hill districts, viz., Karbi Anglong and North Cachar hills. While the major portion of the Hajong population live in the Garo Hills of Meghalaya, a small number of them live in Assam. Apart from the two hill districts, there are a good number of Hajong villages scattered over the plains of Assam in the Brahmaputra valley. In the plain districts of Assam, their main concentration is confined to the Lakhimpur district and in the South Salmara sub-division of Goalpara district. A small number of Hajong families are at present inhabitants of Arunachal Pradesh also. According to their own traditional belief, they originally inhabited the 'Haj paragana' or in Hajo area of present Kamrup district. The Hajongs have their own dialect, which appears to be a mixture of Assamese and Bengali.

In Hajong, a clan is called *nikni*. According to Dr. B. N. Bordoloi, they are divided into seven clans. These clans being exogamous, only at the time of marriage negotiations the concerned families try to trace their clans from oblivion. The Hajongs have a matrilineal family structure and the line of descent is traced through the father only. The father is the head of the family and in all important matters concerning the family his decisions are final. Traditionally Hajongs do not approve marriages between the members of the same clan. They are also very orthodox regarding marriage matters in the sense that no one is allowed to marry outside the community.

The Hajongs were animists like most of the tribal communities of the Northeast. They however, now consider themselves to be Hindus, although some of the traditional religious practices are still found. Hence the religion professed by them at present can be said to be Hinduism combined with their traditional religious practices. The Hajongs believe in various evil spirits like-*Jarang Deo, Machang Deo, Zukhini, Daini, Maila, Bhut*, etc. They worship various Gods and Goddesses like *Durga, Kali, Lakshmi, Kartik, Monosa, Saraswati and Basanti, etc. Kartik puja is known as Katka puja* and *Monosa puja* is known as *Kanideu puja* among the Hajongs. The day of the *Lakshmi puja* is known as the day of '*Kojai Ghar*'. Another important religious worship performed by the Hajongs is '*Kamakhya puja.*

They celebrate their *Bihus*. *Rangali Bihu* (pre-monsoon harvest festival) is known as *Bishuwa* among them. The Hajong villages are situated on high grounds preferably near their wet paddy lands. They construct their dwelling house in clusters in the courtyard of the village headman called '*Adhikari*'. The only prominent house in the village is the house of the *Adhikari*. Like other communities of Assam, rice is the staple food of the Hajongs. Fish is a favourite item of food for them. They don't generally eat pork and fowls. Rice beer brewed at home is a favourite drink but is taken only occasionally. In the performance of socio-religious festivals as well in the performance of rituals rice beer is not used.

The main dress of a Hajong woman is 'patin'. *Patin* is used by women like *mekhala* and it covers the lower part of the body from the waist to the ankle. *Patin* is woven by women at their family looms. Their traditional loom is called '*Bana*' where the use of only two hands is necessary (in many traditional looms found in Assam the feet are used synchronized with the hands). The women cover the upper part of their body with a home woven cotton scarf called *pasra or Agrun* (like that of *chadar* in case of Assamese women).

The men wear a home woven piece of cloth bigger than *Gamosa* (common Assamese hand towel) and it is called *Ningti*.

The primary occupation of the Hajongs is agriculture. The Hajong women are expert weavers. Generally no Hajong house is found without a loom and all women in the household know spinning and weaving. Weaving of cloth in their traditional looms is a household industry. All the clothes required for the female members of a family are produced at the family looms. A significant tradition regarding craft among the Hajongs is that all the clothes needed in the marriage of a girl are required to be woven at the family loom, preferably by the girl herself. There are good carpenters among the Hajongs. They are also expert in manufacturing bamboo and cane goods. Cane and bamboo articles required in a household are produced entirely by the family members, the surplus is sold in the weekly markets.

THE MECHE TRIBE

The Meches are a scheduled tribe in the plain districts of

Assam. The Meches are small in number though. Although their main concentration is found in the Mechapara area of present south Salmara subdivision of the Goalpara district, they are found in small pockets in Khowang area of Dibrugarh district and also in Parakhowa area of the Karbi Anglong district just on the border of the Nagaon District. In Sonitpur district also some Mech villages are there. A good number of Mech families had migrated from the Goalpara district of the Dayang Reserved forest area of Golaghat district also bordering Nagaland and settled area. The Meches are of Tibeto Burman origin and they belong to the great Bodo section of the Tibeto-Burman people. The Meches and the Kacharis are referred to the same stock of people; as they are believed to have a common origin.

The Maches have five principal clans (*Ari*). They are—*Sampramari, Narzinari, Basumatari, Moshariand* and *Hajoari*. In addition to these five principal clans the Maches have other four clans also based on occupations. The clans of the Maches are exogamous and hence the older generation does not approve the marriage within the same clan. The Maches generally marry within their tribe. They follow the partrilineal system of family structure. The line of descent is traced through the father only. The sons inherit property of their father.

Their traditional house contains four huts constructed on the four sides of the courtyard. The houses are built using locally available raw materials like timber, bamboo, thatch, etc. Rice is the staple food of the Maches. Occasionally they take pork, meat of pigeons, fowls, ducks, etc. Formerly they used to take buffalo meat also. Their most favourable drink is rice-beer brewed at home.

Death ceremony is performed in accordance with their customs and traditions on the eight or twelfth day as may be fixed by the village headman in consultation with the village elders.

The religion of the Maches is still in an early stage of transition from animism to Hinduism. They describe themselves as Hindus of the Siva sect and worship Siva called *Batho* and his consort Kali called *Bali Khungri*. The Maches believe that the diseases are caused by the bad spirits. Therefore, cure from ailments are sought through the mysteries of *Ojha* or *Dousi*.

Agriculture is the primary and basic occupation of the Maches. Like the other plain tribes they are also settled cultivators practicing wet-rice cultivation. Animal husbandry plays an important role in their economic life. They rear cows, buffaloes, goats, pigs, fowls, ducks, etc. Women in the families generally look after these animals and birds. Weaving in the family loom and rearing *Erhee* are not only favourite pastimes for women, but are also important cottage industries for them. Most of the domestic requirements of clothes especially for the womenfolk are met from the family looms. Rearing of *Erhee* brings a substantial income to the family. Many families' produce *Erhee* scarves for women as well as for men on their family looms.

The Maches are expert in crafting bamboo and cane

goods. Their domestic requirements are produced by themselves.

THE DIMASA TRIBE

The Dimasa is one of the important ethnic groups of Assam concentrated in North Cachar District of Assam. It belongs to the Bodo stock and the Tibeto-Burman Linguistic family. The term "Dimasa" means the son of big river—*Di* means water *Ma* means big and *Sa*—means son. It may be presumed that the Dimasa consider themselves to be the descendants of the Brahmaputra. According to some scholars Dimasa descended from Hidimba, the princes of Kamrupa who married Bhima (the 2nd Pandaba). This is the only one tribe who had own Kingdom in past and has recorded history. They settled from Dikhuo to Kapili rivers and Dimapur was their Kingdom but due to hostile relationship with Ahom they sifted base to Maibong in NC Hills.

The Dimasa spread in four territorial divisions of Assam:

- *Hassao* — N. C. Hills.
- *Hawar* — Plains of Cachar District (Bammans).
- *Dembra* — In and around Hojai, Lanka, Kharani and Hawraghat.
- *Dijowa* — Dhansiri, Mohungdijua and Dimapur.

In the N. C. Hills the Dimasas are dwelling mainly in Hamri-Langting, Wargongsa-Mandardisa, Semsa-Semkhar, and in Hasaopure—Maibong. The Dimasas constitute almost 15 per cent of total population of NC hills and 2.45 per cent of total Scheduled Tribes population of Assam.

The Dimasas follow the patriarchal system of family structure and father is the head of the family. They have significant existence of 42 female clans (*Zaluk*) parallel to 40 male clans (*Sengphong*). All clans are exogamous and marriage between boys and girls of same clan is prohibited. Marriage by negotiation is the prevailing practice but marriage by elopement or capture is also found. The bride price 'kalti' is also a regular practice.

They cremate the body of the dead on the bank of a River or stream. During the death ceremony, the villagers and relatives are to be entertained with a feast.

Paternal property like real estates, weapons, cash, and cattle are inherited by sons and the maternal property—jewelry, cloths, looms—goes to daughters and other common property is divided equally between sons & daughters.

In Dimasa the Village system is called *Nablai*, which means a cluster of houses. The entire village with its population is called *Raji* and they generally prefer the hill slopes near a stream. The rural houses have timber superstructure, mud-plastered bamboo walls and thatched roofs. They are artistically designed and are built on two rows facing each other and leaving sufficient space in between. The houses are built on ground and protected by bamboo wall from strong wind. Each village has protective fencing all round the village.

Kunang is the traditional head man of the Dimasa village, and he settles the disputes with the help of assistant headman *Dilo* and other elder members of the village. The *Nodrang* (bachelor dormitory) act as an important institution of their cultural life, responsible for protection of village, social functions and works.

Agriculture is their principal source of livelihood. Both wet land and *Jhum* forms are practiced. They also rear buffaloes, pig, goats, fowls and ducks. The weaving and crafting of cane and bamboo products also are traditional expertise of the Dimasas.

The rice is their staple food and an average Dimasa takes the same thrice daily with vegetables, meat, fish. The *Zou* is their traditional rice beer. They use tea without milk as a beverage.

The Dimasa is a colourful tribe. They have five indigenous musical instruments namely *Khram* (dram) *Muri, Muri Wathisa, Suphin* (all flutes made form reed and bamboo), *Khram Dubung* (an instrument like veena). They have numerous folklore and tales and they perform dance and songs in their festivals. The *Busu* is their harvesting festival where the people make a specially designed gate—*fangsla* in the entrance of the village. *Rajini Gabra* and *Harni Gabra* are socio-religious festivals held once annually before the starting of cultivation.

The Dimasa have their traditional dress and ornaments. The male folk use generally deep green coloured *Risa* (Dhuti), shirt, beautiful scarf (*Rinsao*), cotton or Erhee silk turban and long shirt like overcoat with silver earring (*Kharih*) and armlets (*Youcher*). On the other hand the women put on cotton or erhee skirt (*Rigu*), scarf (*Rijamphai*) for upper part of body and another scarf (*Rikhaosa*) during dance. They also use *Chandrawal, Poal, Rongborsa* (silver made necklace) *Khamontai* (golden earrings), *Khadu* (heavy silver bracelet), *Eansidam* (nose ring), *Khamonhai* (silver earring) *Liksim*, *Likjao* and *Jongsama* (necklaces).

They have thick calves, broad head, stumpy noses, thick lips, languish eyes and prominent check bones. Their complexion is almost dark-tan.

In due course of time many changes took place among the Dimasas in their traditional life. They are now managing their own affairs, which have enabled them to be politically conscious and also to look after their own development and welfare.

THE TIWAS (LALUNGS)

The Lalungs prefer to call themselves as Tiwa, an important tribe of Assam specially concentrated in the Morigaon District. It belongs to the great Bodo race and Tibeto-Burman linguistic family. They are medium stature, strong built and generally white complexioned people with flat nose, straight hair, wide faces, scanty beards and moustaches—the features of Mongoloids.

La means water and *Lung* means rescued. The river Brahmaputra gave shelter to these Bohemian people, hence they were Lalungs. Mythically they were originated from the saliva (Lal) of lord Siva. In the word Tiwa *Ti* means water and *Wa* means superior. As the Lalungs landed on plains following the river Brahmaputra, they introduced themselves as Tiwa. According to the scholars, Tiwa derives from the term Tibbatia meaning the people hailing from Tibet. Originally, it is believed that they also came down from Tibet to Jayantia Hills and then migrated to Central Assam and then established *Gobha* kingdom. The Tiwas are spread through Mayang, Bhurbandha, Kathiatali, Kampur area of Greater Nagaon in central Assam, and in some villages in Titabor, Dhemaji, Sonapur, Nartiang Elaka of Jowai in Meghalaya, foot hills of Karbi Anglong District.

Agriculture is the principal occupation. Individual or community fishing is prevalent in their society. Barter system is still being adored and practiced in their society. During Jonbil Mela (kind of a selling and buying festival held every year in January) the Tiwas and other tribes exchange their produces with others products in a barter system.

The rice is their staple food. Fish, meat (pork, fowl, ducks), vegetables, eggs are also included in the menu. Tea without milk and *Zu* (rice beer) are their beverages. They collect their supplementary food (stem, root, leaves) and fire woods from the nearest forest.

The Tiwas in the plain construct their houses on plinth, and in the hills on traditional pattern on plinths. Traditionally thatch has been used for roofing. The walls of the traditional houses are made of reeds and bamboo. Generally they use wooden or bamboo posts and make three rooms—*Barghar* for Kitchen 2/3 feet above the ground, *Majarghar* (bed room) and *Soraghar* (living-cum-guest room). The unmarried children are also accommodated in the *Soraghar*. The granary for the plain Tiwas is constructed towards east; the hill Tiwas keep their grains in a big container made by barks of tree (*Kerehi*).

The women folk are experts in weaving and almost every household possesses loom. Knowledge of weaving is a traditional qualification for marriageable damsels. The women *wear Mekhala, Chadar, Riha, Kingkhap, Sondia Kapor, Thenus* (Chadar), *Seleng, Sakathia* and *Farke* (blouse) they also wear *Man Kapor, Bor Kapor* and *Tongali* (waist band) during festivals with ornaments like *Gamkharu, Sipatmani* (necklace), *Gotakharu* (bracelet) *Sen Patia Angathi* (ring). Men put on *Nimai* shirt and *Thagla* with earring (*Siha*). Hill Tiwas put on a *Lengti, Tangali* and decorative threads *Dahi*. The traditional Tiwa King (the concept of kingdom still exists among the Tiwa and the King traditionally inaugurates the *Jonbil Mela*) wears Muga *dhoti* and shirt and headgear made of cloth (*Paguri*), cotton Chadar, silver necklace, *gamkharu*, earring, Other ornaments the King traditionally carries are *Langkor* (sword), *aaron, Bisani* (hand fan), silver pot, *Thona* and *Nisan.*

Tiwas are exceptional in expressing their artistic talents through innumerable textile designs. Both floral and geometrical designs are popular among them. They are also experts in cane and bamboo works. Cane baskets of various designs are widely used by the womenfolk. Other products like *Japa* (suitcase), *pera* (big suitcase made of wood), *petari* (small suitcase) *Sarai, Bota* (elevated wooden plates) are specialties of the male artisans. They also make canoes, wooden spinning wheel and masks. Carving of animals and birds are seen in the entrance beam of the *Samadi* (dormitory) and carved elephant designs in combs. The Tiwas have own blacksmiths in Kamarkuchi village near Jagiroad who are said to have made cannons and swords for the ancient kings. The carved stone and metal works are also displayed in various places of Nagaon district.

The Tiwas are lovers of music. The three varieties of Drums *Khrambarv* (big drum), *Pisu Khram* (small) and *Khram, b*amboo made Flutes, *Kali* (pipe), *Tandrang* (violin like string instrument), *Thogari* (string instrument) are traditionally being produced locally.

The Tiwa society is a stratified society and there are different office bearers in a village. However, structural differences are not prevalent in Tiwa society except for socio-religious occasions. The *Buni* is a small unit of village administration. *Gaonburha* assisted by *Barik, Changdoloi, Changmaji, Huruma* and *Khuramul* is responsible for village administration. The *Deori* is responsible for worship. *Deo Raja* is how the traditional king is known as, and *Bordoloi, Konwar, Patra, Barbarua,* etc. are some office bearers of the kingdom. A typical Tiwa village has 20 to 40 houses. It has *Samadi* (dormitory) traditionally for training youths in art, crafts and in musical lore and to prepare them to take responsibility of the village administration. However, now-a-days the dormitory is converted into a public hall and no longer bachelors are found taking training in it. Community prayer hall is also found in every village.

Tiwa family structure is nuclear type but some times old parents and unmarried brothers and sisters also live together. In case of plain Tiwas the properties inherently go to sons only and divided equally but in case of matrilineal Hills Tiwa the mother's property is inherited by the daughters. They have 12 clans and several sub-clans under one clan. Clan exogamy is strictly adhered to and monogamy is socially recognised. There are four forms of marriage—*Bor Biya, Gobhia Rakha, Joron Biya and Poluai Ana* (elopement). A nominal bride price may also be seen among some clans.

Hill Tiwas worship a stone image. Both cremation and burial are in practice in Tiwa society. On the 3rd or 7th days of death small feasts are arranged for purification. The *Karam* is solemnising in grand manner after 5/6 years.

The Tiwa have elaborate socio-religious festivals *like Bisu, Barat, Sagra, Misawa, Wansua/Wanzua* including the *Jonbil Mela* where they perform dances and songs with instruments. *LaHai* and *Lali Hilali* are the songs used to celebrate most of the occasions.

REFERENCES

Bhattacharyya, P. C. (ed) (1962), *Asomor Janajati.* Jorhat, Asom Sahitya Sabha.

Baruah, S. K. (2004), Tribes of Assam, *Assam Year Book 2004*, Guwahati, Jyoti Prakashan.

Bordoloi B. N., Sharmathakur, G. C. and Saikia M. C. (1987), *Tribes of Assam* (Vol. I) Guwahati, Tribal Research Institute, Assam.

Bordoloi, B. N. (1991), *Tribes of Assam*, Guwahati, Assam Institute of Research for Tribal and Scheduled Cast.

Bordoloi, B. (1972), Lalung Jatir Parichay, *Ringsang,* 1(1).

Gait, Sir Edward (1929), *A History of Assam*, Guwahati, Lawyers Book Stall.

Ghosh, G. K. (1992), *Tribals and Their Culture, Volume I*, New Delhi: Ashish Publishing House.

Mipun, J. (1993), *The Mishings of Assam*, New Delhi, Gyan Publishing House.

Pula, M. L. (2000), *Tribal India: Communities, Customs and Culture*, New Delhi, Dominant Publishers and Distributors.

Sengupta, S. (1996), *People of Northeast India*, New Delhi, Gyan Publishing House

Singh, A. K. (1993), *Tribes and Tribal Life*, New Delhi, Swarup & Sons.

Singh, K. S. (1994), *The Scheduled Tribes*, New Delhi, Oxford University Press.

Waddell, L. A. (1975), *The Tribes of The Brahmaputra Valley*, New Delhi, Logos Press.

4

Objectives and Methodology

Souvenir buying is an integral part of travel. As mentioned in the earlier chapters no tour is complete without the purchase of souvenirs from the visiting destinations. From the point of view of 'looking back with nostalgia' tourists like to buy souvenirs which are endemic, unique and authentic to the destinations. As discussed in Chapter 2 crafts of a region are the true representative of the uniqueness of the destination, which the tourists can take back with them as a tangible memory of the visit.

North East India, particularly Assam has abundance of tourism resources and of late the number of tourists visiting the region has been increasing steadily. Many of those who chose to visit Assam may seek some novel experience in terms of wild life and the cultural heritage of the large number of ethnic groups living here. These tourists are not necessarily mass tourists and therefore, in all probability they would like to seek the 'alternative ways' of touristic experience. This calls for detailed discussion and exposure of the alternative forms of products that could be offered to the visiting tourists. As the marketing literature has always been emphasising that the products which are being offered must appeal to the prospective buyers and should be valued by them. Thus the need of the hour is to record the tourism products that can be developed for touristic consumption, which are unique to the State or to a particular destination within the state.

Craft might be one of such distinguishable products which could be developed. The entire NE region is very rich in craft works and every nook and corner of this region can boast of skilled and gifted craft workers. Therefore, it is felt necessary to document the crafts of the state of Assam which might be thrown open in a more formal way for the touristic experience. Even though we are aware that Assam is rich in craft works no authentic document is available as a package for the tourists' consumption. In view of this need the following objectives for the present study have been set. Care have been taken to address the need of the tourists from the marketing point of view and thus the objectives might not reflect all the requirements of the study that would have been directed to craft documentation only.

OBJECTIVES

1. The study tries to bring out craft products which are unique and authentic to a region within the state of Assam.
2. The study envisages to document regions identified as a result of the objective number 1 so that the same could be offered to the tourists in a package.
3. Propose certain travel circuits encompassing the famous destinations with few craft producing regions.

SCOPE

The study encompasses only the traditional craft products of the region. This is done in order to exploit only the authentic crafts of the region. Thus only the areas traditionally known for a particular craft have been included in the purview of the study.

While defining craft the following modified version of the definition given by Yavary (1992) is adopted:

Handicraft can be defined as the combination of art and craft, where local raw materials are used in the process of production; the main stages of production are performed by hand with manual tools and instruments; and each product unit reflects its producer's artistic talent and mental creativity in some way. The characteristics the handicraft possesses are as follows:

1. Some main stages of production being done by hand, and by manual tools and instruments;
2. The effective presence of human creativity in production and formation of manufactured products with diversity of designs and the techniques of carrying them out,
3. The utilisation of the main part of raw material(s), from the domestic resources;
4. Having cultural weight;
5. Dissimilarity of productive outputs with one another; and
6. Capability of being established and developed in techniques of production for generations.

As the definition suggests all those having artistic expression and made by hand are not crafts for the purpose of the study. Thus the scope of the study will exclude the pure artistic hand made items like fine arts (painting by artists, etc.) as the same do not fulfill the characteristics mentioned in the serial number (6).

LIMITATION

As the scope and objectives suggests the study suffers from certain limitations in terms of scope. The crafts which have emerged as a result of commercialisation are not taken into consideration. The commercial centres of craft production, which are artificial in nature and do not fulfill the criteria at serial no. (6) above, are not taken into account. Thus certain urban centres where craft festivals are held or brisk craft transactions take place are kept beyond the reach of this research.

Production process including designing is not studied in this research. A study on this aspect needs a lot of expertise in the textile and craft design and production and hence the same was kept beyond the scope of this research; the objectives also do not require this.

Extant knowledge of the craft works of different regions of the state was used while deciding to include certain areas in the study. Thus all regions of the state may not have representation in this study.

The study takes the craft works from the point of view

of touristic marketing only. Therefore, the obvious areas included here had to fulfill two criteria. (1) Tourists should have easy accessibility to this area, and (2) Proper infrastructure like accommodation should be available in the vicinity. These criteria pose as limitations of the study as few areas might be left behind the scope of this study.

While describing the tribes indigenous to Assam, an exhaustive list of such tribes could not be drawn. This is because of the fact that only major tribes are outlined and the information were taken from secondary sources, as the primary objective of this work is only to map the craft of Assam.

METHODOLOGY

In a field-work based qualitative study deciding about a perfect methodology is a tough task. Social scientists have engaged in different methods for documenting the field-level findings. Focus on group interview, in-depth interviews, observation and documentation are few such widely used methods.

As the objectives suggest this study calls for a careful selection of research methodology so that basic purpose of conducting it could be fulfilled.

Data Sources

Secondary Sources: For the purpose of tourism related

information various secondary sources were used. The sources were mainly books, reports and brochures and write-ups. The detailed list of all such sources is reproduced in the Bibliography.

Primary Information: Structured in-depth interviews were conducted with 172 knowledgeable persons. The respondents were selected on the basis of their knowledge-base regarding the crafts in a particular locality. They are basically craftsmen or proprietors of various craft related business organisations. The interviewees were basically selected to gain knowledge about a craft work and also to gain insight on the places where these craftsmen are concentrated traditionally. They are selected on the basis of judgment in the region itself or during different craft festivals. For example, Mr. Hitlal Kalita, a celebrated textile worker from Sualkuchi was selected for the purpose. In Sarthebari, Mr. Subhas Tamuli, Secretary of Assam Samabay Kanhar Sangha, was selected as a respondent and the in-depth interview was conducted. The whole process of data collection went on for the year 2005 and the better part of 2006. The detailed list of the respondents is offered towards the end of this chapter.

The number of respondents selected in different regions is shown in the following Table 4.1.

The respondents were basically asked about the concentration of traditional crafts, the production process and the problems & prospects related with the craft.

Table 4.1: Region-wise in-depth Interview on Related Craft

Geographical Region	*Number of Respondents*	*Related Craft*
Hajo	21	Brass Metal work
Sualkuchi	14	Muga and Mulberry Textile
Sarthebari	19	Bell Metal work
Nalbari	05	Cane and bamboo works, Erhee Textile
Barpeta	12	Ivory work and Cane and Bamboo work
Bangaigaon	06	Cane and Bamboo works
Kokrajhar	16	Cotton, Erhee and Muga Textile, Cane and Bamboo works
Asharkandi	10	terracota
Gauripur	4	Sola pith
Goalpara	12	Sital pati
Lakhimpur, Dhemaji	32	Cotton, Erhee Textile, craft
Jonai		Cotton, Erhee Textile
Karbi Anglong	08	Bamboo and cane works, textile
North Cachar Hills	08	Bamboo and cane works, textile
Festivals and fares	05	Bamboo and cane works, textile
TOTAL	**172**	

Detailed documentation is done basically on the type of craft produced in these areas, local names, accessibility and available infrastructure.

In many cases direct observations were also conducted for getting a feel of the craft that was being produced. Specially, observations were made in Sualkuchi, Kokjrajhar, Hajo, Sarthebari, Lakhimpur, Dhemaji and Jonai regions. In the North Cachar Hill District and also in some pockets of Karbi Anglong district direct observation was not possible because of the presence of extremist groups in the rural areas and thus the primary data collection process could be limited to only in-depth-interviews with some knowledgeable persons in the vicinity. This may also be treated as a limitation to the study.

Region-Wise Respondents for In-Depth Interviews

Sipajar Craft Festival (Sahitya Sabha, 2005)

1. Dadhi Pathak, Renowned Craftsman
2. Ramani Kanta Deka
3. Balaram Rabha, Textile
4. Sewali Rabha
5. Atikur Rahman, Woodcraft

HAJO

1. Ghanashyam Ojha
2. Kakhiram Deka
3. Ashok Hatkhota Kutir Udyod
4. Rajid Ali

5. Saifuddin Ahmed
6. Khalek Ali
7. Nabi Hussain
8. Seikh Sarmat Ali
9. Pradip Das
10. Upen Pathak
11. Barendra Das
12. Satya Bharali
13. Nayan Ch Das
14. Bibek Das
15. Nagen Das
16. Kandarpa Das
17. Dimbeswar Das
18. Deben Bharali
19. Dwijen Nayak
20. Arup Nayak
21. Bhadreswar Nayak

Sualkuchi

1. Chandan Kumar Moral
2. Paresh Baishya
3. Bipul Medhi
4. Hemanta Kumar
5. Dhiren Kalita
6. Nilamani Sarma
7. Hitlal Kalita Renowned Craftsman
8. Kanika Kalita
9. Dipali Bora
10. Bipul Das
11. Manoj Das

12. Pratima Kalita
13. Bhaity Kalita
14. Dhiraj Baishya

Sarthebari

1. Beswanath Deka
2. Pramod Chandra Barman
3. Pranab CH Barman
4. Niranajan Barman
5. Haliram Barman
6. Jogesh CH Baishya
7. Umesh CH Deka
8. Abhay Deka
9. Kamini Deka
10. Dhiren Deka
11. Tapan Deka
12. Abhi Bhuyan
13. Kamalkanta Choudhury
14. Parikshit Deka
15. Bhabesh Talukdar
16. Bhagaban Deka
17. Kalpa Bhuyan
18. Satay Deka
19. Subhas Tamuli, Secy. ASSAM Samabay Kahar Sangha

Barpeta

1. Sailen Das Rajnath Ivory Art House
2. Hridayanda Das
3. Alakesh Das

4. Tiken Bhuyan
5. Mahibul Hussain, Handicraft Designer—Saptarshi Handicraft
6. Sultana Nazia Rahman, Naz Handicraft
7. Pradeep Das, Assam Hastasilpa Kendra
8. Manabendra Deka, Deka Cane And Bamboo
9. Nazmin Alam
10. Imran Hussain
11. Matiur Rahman, Al-Amin Rual Welfare Society
12. Gopesh Das, Das Handicraft

Bangaigaon

1. Subodh Pal, Subodh Silpalaya
2. Pradip Pal, Trinath Silpa Kutir
3. Tapan Pal
4. Bhumidahr Sinha, Cane Works
5. Amir Ali
6. Phultan Ahmed

Kokrajhar

1. Mandip Rup Bikram Brahma, Secy, Bodoland Association of Handloom Units, Renowed For Textile Work Emplying 100 Weavers
2. Malati Narzary
3. Ms Milan Narzary, Milan Industry
4. Chaya Brahma Choudhury, Ms Chaya Industries
5. Ramani Basumatary, Ramani Industry
6. Maldang Basumatary, Zayclong Industry
7. Ms Rimwnla Basumatary
8. Ms Lashmi Basumatary

9. Ms Jaymati Bargayary
10. Ms Mitu Basumatary
11. Ms Sunila Basumatary

Chirang District, No.1 Saljora Village

12. Lalmohan Basumatary
13. Sambara Basumatary
14. Churamani Basumatary
15. Ms. Arunima Mushahary
16. Ms. Noni Mushahary

Asharikandi

1. Dhirendra Nath Pal
2. Mahadev pal,
3. Bishu pada pal, Secy. Asharikandi terracota dol making samabay samity limited.
4. Baloram Pal, Chairman
5. Ramdulal Pal
6. Chittaranjan Pal
7. Amulya Pal
8. Ranjit Pal
9. Subal Pal
10. Nimai Pal

Sola Pith Village (Gauripur)

1. Md Zakkir Hussain, Secy., Dhubri Hastasilpa Samabay Samity Limited
2. Narendra Malakar
3. Karen Malakar
4. Dulal Malakar

Goalpara

1. Gobinda Nandi
2. Ranjit Dey
3. Dilip Dey
4. Ananda Pal
5. Manikanta Dey
6. Ajit Nandi
7. Gobinda Dey

New Dubapara

8. Biren Pal
9. Jagdish Pal
10. Ananda Pal
11. Arjun Pal
12. Dulal Pal

Lakhimpur, Dhemaji

1. Ms Mileswari Doley, Moon Industry, Chetiya Gaon
2. Ms Najitara Bori, Karpumpuli Industry
3. Ms Damayanti Pame, Kangkan Industry
4. Ms Sunity Pame, Kangkin Industry
5. Ms Konari Dole Pegu, Amiya Industry

Ghagar

6. Kachari Doley
7. Tulsi Pegu
8. Kangkonk Taid
9. Biren Doley
10. Santiram Doely
11. Jiban Mili

12. Harendra Doley

Ghunasuti

13. Prabhat Panging
14. Rajen Taid
15. Tankeswar Taid
16. Kamaleswar Taid
17. Dulal Mili
18. Rajeswar Mili

Gogamukh

19. Chenimai Doley (Winner Of Best Craft Designer Award At National and State Level)
20. Champabati Doley, Secy.
21. Durgeswari Doley Pegu, President Kankank Samabai Samity
22. Gimi Pegu, Pegu Industries
23. Takar Doely
24. Mokhya patir, Rtd. Principal gogamukh H S school
25. Dinamohan Doely, Lecturer Gogamukh College
26. Muhiram Pegu
27. Santiram Doely, President, Gaon Panchayat

Dhemaji

28. Urmila Mili, Mili's Industries

Jonai

29. Nanda Pal Doley
30. Upeswar Doley
31. Chandra Nath Doely

Bahir Jonai

32. Bijay Saikia

Haflong

1. Dr Dipak Nath
2. Hemanta Chutia
3. Secy. Dimasa Students Union
4. Biju Hadger, Deprtment of Culture and Information
5. Ms Purnam, Zeme Cyultural Society, Bora Halflong
6. Bhaben Langthasa, Craft Busienssman
7. Ms S K Singh, Halflong Craft Market
8. K D Dangalapa

Karbi Anglong

1. Ms Purnima Terron Larangthasa
2. Ms Kamalini
3. Ashim Bora
4. President Karbi Cultural Society
5. Purna Terron, Karbi Cultural Society
6. Rongbong Terang, Educationist, Diphu
7. Gautam Roy
8. D Kalita, Journalist

5

Handicrafts and Assam

Assam is vibrant and very rich in handicraft and handloom products. Specially, handloom from Assam is world famous and the handmade textiles of the state have been a matter of discussion from the time of the *Puranas*.

WEAVING

Weaving is a way of life in Assam. Almost every house in the village has the prized possession of a loom. The Muga, Pat (mulberry) and Erhee (Endi) are the three different types of handmade natural fabrics. These have been used extensively in the local handloom industry. The Muga threads, made from cocoons of Muga are found only in China's southern provinces except in Assam. However, this craft has recently been adopted by some neighbouring areas like north Bengal. This thread is golden in colour and popularly known as the '*golden thread*'. In Assam an estimated 50 crore muga cocoons are harvested every year, and about 95 per cent of these are used for reeling threads. Mulberry is also available elsewhere in the country but Assam's mulberry is unique in richness and is made of natural process. Erhee or Endi is endemic to few districts of lower and central Assam and this type of warm natural yarn is found no where in the world. This makes

Assam's handloom industry unique in the world, and the textiles produced in the looms of Assam are sought after all over the world, specially in the developed countries where naturalism has become the lifestyle of the rich and the wealthy. The name of the village Sualkuchi is worth mentioning here as hundreds of looms are helping keeping up the tradition alive and kicking in the most professional way.

In general the production of natural fabrics passes through three unique stages—warm rearing-cum-cocoon production, spinning and weaving. Many regional pockets of Assam have developed specialty in these three components for different fabrics. This specialisation might be attributed to the distinguished knowledge endemic to the region passes on by generations of craftsmen. The environmental suitability also plays a major role in region specific concentration.

The major areas which have specialisation in these stages of the three distinguished threads are as shown in Table 5.1. The regions are also depicted in Map 2: Assam-Textile Producing Regions.

The State has concentration for general cotton weaving also. Such prominent places include whole of BTC areas (Bodo dominated), Nalbari, Darrang district, North and Eastern Sonitpur district, all areas dominated by Mishing people (specially Lakhimpur, Dhemaji and Majuli areas), Morigaon area, Karbi Anglong and North Cachar hills.

Table 5.1: Region-Wise Concentration of Textile Producing in Assam

	Muga	*Erhee*	*Mulberry*
Warm Rearing and Cocoon production	Dhemaji, Dhakuakhana, Lahimpur, Tinsukia, Boko, Mirza, Dibrugarh, Jorhat, Golaghat, Sualkuchi, Goalpara	Dhemaji, Lakhimpur, Dibrugarh, Majuli, Karbi Anglong region, Marigaon, NC Hills, Silchar, Karimganj, Hailakandi, Jagiroad, Mirza, Goalpara, Kokrajhar, Bangaigaon, Bodoland Territorial Council region, Nalbari, Darrang, Sonitpur	Jorhat, Darrang
Spinning	Sualkuchi, Palashbari, Kokrajhar	-do-	Sualkuchi, Kokrajhar
Weaving	Sualkuchi, Kokrajhar	-do-	Sualkuchi, Kokrajhar

Source: Silk Map of North east India (Central Silk Technological research Institute) and Field survey.

JEWELRY

Jewelry, particularly of gold is a tradition in Assam. The Sonowal Kachari tribe collected gold from the beds of the rivers flowing down the Himalayas in the ancient times. The jewellers known as Sonari make exquisite *Doog-Doogi*,

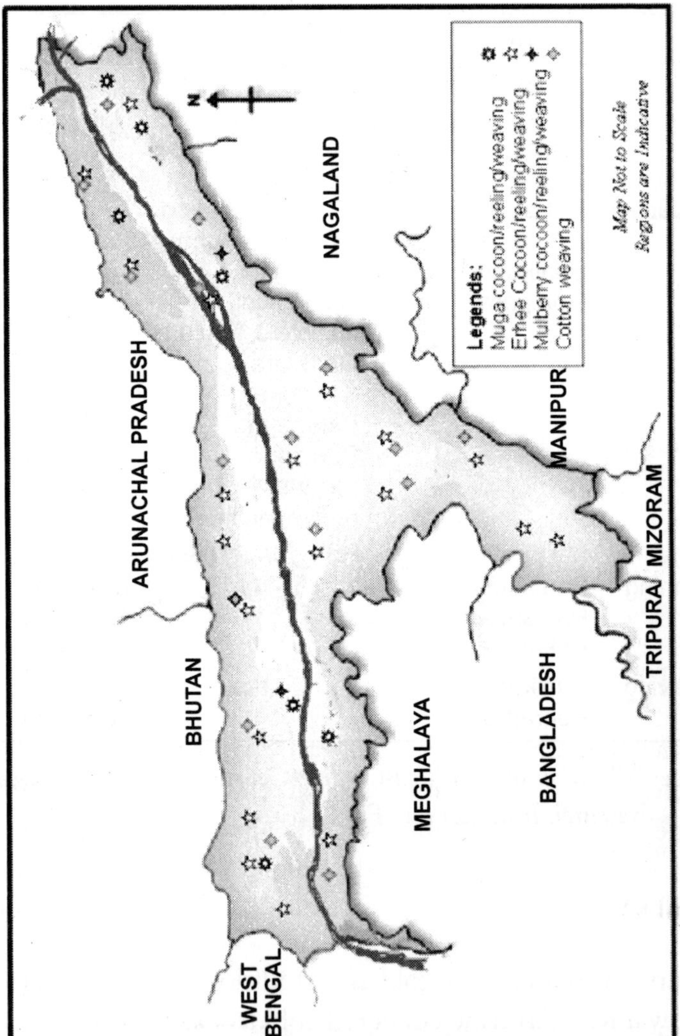

Map 2: Assam— Textile Producing Regions

Bana, Jon-biri, Dhol-biri type lockets; *Thuriya, Loka-paro* and *Keru* earrings; *Gaam-kharu* (bracelets) and *Gal-pata* (necklaces). The Karonga area of Jorhat district is famous for its artisans those can craft beautiful and exotic cane and gem jewelry.

BRASS AND BELL METAL

Brass and Bell Metal products are famous for their beauty, strength and utility. In Hajo of Kamrup district Brass is an important cottage industry. Sarthebari in the same district is famous for bell metal crafts. The artisans traditionally manufacture *Kalah* (water pot), *Sarai, Kahi* (dish) *Bati* (bowl), *Lota* and *Tal* (cymbals). The traditional hand made dinner set of bell metal is breathtaking and even today the bell metal utensils are used in honour of the visiting guest.

POTTERY AND TERRACOTTA

Assam is also famous for its exotic **pottery** works. Household articles, toys, dolls and images of worship are the favourites of the pottery artists in Assam. Goalpara district of lower Assam is famous for its earthen dolls made of *terracotta.* ***Kuhila*** (Sola) or Indian cork is also used for doll making and for decorative purposes. However, this particular fiber has also been used traditionally in *Sattra*s (vaishnavite monasteries) of Assam for weaving mats and cushions.

*Sattra*s are also testimonies of bygone era of wood

carvings of Assam. Exquisite wood carvings are seen in the doors, walls, beams, and ceilings and also in the temples of the *Sattras*. The *Singhasanas* or the vaishnavite shrines are made of wood and the carvings of the shrines are equally mind-boggling. The Tezpur ghat indicates that a large number of boats in the Brahmaputra were carved with beautiful designs and decorated with ornaments. Wood was used for the making of icons, as proved by an icon of Jagannatha in Khetri in modern Kamrup. Speaking of the various articles of wood, a later source Fathiyah-i-Ibriyah narrates about wooden boxes, stools, trays and chairs that were made from a single piece of wood. The wood carvers of the present generation have concentrated on devising some traditional and modern art forms so that a ready-made demand can be exploited.

Assam is rich in sylvan resources and most of its forests are richly stocked with bamboo and canes of various species. In bamboo and reeds, Assam has the most concentrated forests in the whole of India. As many as 51 species of bamboo grow in Assam. Bamboo is a raw material of great versatility and forms an integral part of the lifestyle and economy of Assam. The making of bamboo and cane products is perhaps the most universal of all the crafts practiced by a large number of artisans scattered throughout the State. It is practiced as a household industry and no mechanical device is used. Cane and bamboo products are used for a wide range of purposes and extensively used in every household. Assam has probably the maximum resources for the cane and bamboo industry in India comparable with Canada and the Scandinavian countries-Sweden, Norway and Finland (IGNCA, 1999).

CANE AND BAMBOO

Various types of *cane and bamboo* products are found in this state. The people of the plain and hill districts of Assam have their own bamboo and cane products with distinctive features and typical designs. The products of the plain districts differ from those of the hill districts in use, shape and design. It is found that a variety of products like bamboo mats, *sital pati,* baskets of various sizes and shapes, winnowing trays, sieves, *japi* or umbrella, storage materials like *khorahi, Duli, Dukla,* etc. are manufactured in large numbers in the plain districts of the state. The cane and bamboo products used for domestic purposes are prepared in every nook and corner of the state out of split bamboo and fine flexible cane strips. The cane furnisher of Assam is world famous and a large number of artisans are earning their livelihood working in such cottage industries.

There are various kinds of *fishing traps* prepared out of cane and bamboo in different parts of the state. Some of the fishing implements like *polo, Jakai, Khalai, Dori, Chepa, Paran, Jhuti, Hogra,* etc. are widely used.

Different types of *bamboo and cane mates* (*Dhari* and *Pati*) are also very popular in Assam, specially in the rural area and thousands of artisans are engaged in producing these. *Japi* deserves a special mention as this particular handicraft has caught the attention of the country as a whole. There are two distinct types of *japi*. One is for day-to-work in the field that is basically used by the farmers; and the other one is for decorative purposes, which was once used by the kings, queens and nobles of the *Ahom* kingdom. The later variety is now-a-days improvised incorporating different colours and designs and almost all household of the state, be it in a rural area or in an urban area possesses this variety of *japi* as wall-hanging. Thus *japi* has a very high potential for being promoted as a tourism product along with other handmade items of bamboo and cane. Nalbari district of lower Assam is famous for different types of *Japi*. A detailed area wise discussion is offered hereafter.

SUALKUCHI (A TEXTILES VILLAGE)

Sualkuchi is famous for its Muga and mulberry textiles. Main advantage of this village is that the tourist can have a comprehensive one-stop experience of the weaving technology and process of these two famous textiles of Assam. Though the weavers across the state can make mulberry and Muga textiles the gifted weavers of this village are famous for their craftsmanship, professionalism and profitability. Thus there is no wonder that the village flourishes as a textile hub of not only Assam but of the whole of North-east India. Numerous cooperatives of weavers are working relentlessly along with privately owned looms to upkeep their traditional spot in hand weaving in the region. No visit to Assam is complete without a tour to this magnificent village.

Photo Plate 1: Textile Designs

Design of a Cotton *Chadar*

Flower and Diamond Designs of a Mulberry *Chadar*

Elephant and Bird Designs

- *Location*: Sualkuchi is situated in the north bank of the Brahmaputra in Kamrup district at a distance of 32 km from Guwahati. Regular and frequent bus services are available to and from Guwahati. Buses charge only Rs. 8.00 from Guwahati and time taken is about 55 min. Taxi service is also available; taxi charges about Rs. 600.00 to drop at Sualkuchi.
- *Accommodation facility*: There is no accommodation facility at Sualkuchi for outside visitor. Visitor can accommodate themselves at Guwahati.
- *Craft and the local people*: Sualkuchi's mulberry and Muga (golden cloths) textiles are famous in the world. The mulberry and Muga cloths are woven by local weavers without using power loom. In Sualkuchi about 95 per cent of the inhabitants are directly or indirectly related with the silk industry. In Sualkuchi about 3500 silk production units and about 10000 looms are working at present. Now-a-days different types of new designs are made with the help of computer, but this computerised design is not able to decrease the popularity of traditional design. And the designers are also interested to conserve the traditional design. Some of the traditional designs are named as follows—*miri, magar, kinkhap*, etc. These designs include pictures of temples, animals, geometrical shapes, and sometimes natural scenery too.

  Some of the designs consist of sprays of flowers and elephants interspersed with leaves and springs, and numerous combinations of geometrical patterns.

- *Economics*: One Mulberry and Muga production cum selling unit sells for up to Rs. 1 Lakh per month. The price of the finished product varies between Rs. 3000.00-3500.00 for a set of Muga *Mekhala chadar* and Rs. 5000.00 to Rs. 7000.00 for a set of pure Mulberry. However, the price shoots up during the marriage seasons of April to June and of October to December. Traditionally in every Assamese marriage the bride is to be presented with a number of Muga and Mulberry sets, and hence the increase in price.
  The weavers are paid reasonably, and during 2006 their earnings were as shown below.
  For one piece of cloth (*Sadar*) Rs. 300.00 (minimum) for one piece of (*Mekhala*) Rs.150.00 (minimum) and For one piece of *Saree* Rs. 500.00 (minimum)
- *Raw materials*: Mulberry yarn is mainly brought from Banglore and Mysore in the form of reeled yarn. Muga is brought in the form of cocoons from different local producers of Lakhimpur, Dhakuakhana, Boko, Mirza, Palashbari and also from the Garo hills of Meghalaya. From Muga cocoons silk yarn is extracted by reeling method. Muga reeling is unwinding of filament from cocoons combining 8 to 12 filaments together and getting a thread suitable for weaving of cloth. One kg of reeled yarn can be recovered from 5000 quality cocoons. One kg of reeled quality silk yarn costs around Rs. 5000.00 at the market price of 2006.

Total annual output of Muga raw silk is only around 100 tons and more than 90 per cent of it comes from Assam.

HAJO (A BRASS METAL VILLAGE)

Hajo is situated on the north bank of the Brahmaputra, in Kamrup district of Assam, at a distance of 24 km from Guwahati. Regular city bus services are available to and from Guwahati. City buses charge only Rs. 8 from Guwahati and time taken is about 45 minutes. Taxi service is also available. Taxi charges Rs. 400.00 to Rs. 500.00 to drop at Hajo.

Accommodation: There is a tourist lodge at Hajo run by Assam Tourism Development Corporation (ATDC). There are four rooms, two are three bedded and the rest are four bedded.

- *Main Crafts of the local people*: Hajo is well known for its Brass-metal artisans. Works on brass metal is an old traditional craft of this area. From brass metal different types of utensils and materials of daily needs have been crafted by skilled craftsmen for generations. In Hajo more than 35 families are related with this craft. It is estimated that in a typical day 70 craftsmen produce almost 140 brass metal craft. The average annual production thus touches almost 48 ton.

  Brass metal workers belong to both major communities of the village, Hindu and Muslim. The

Photo Plate 2: Brass and Bell Metal Works

Some Traditional Brass and Bell Metal Works Preserved at a *Sattra*

Finished Brass Metal Pitchers

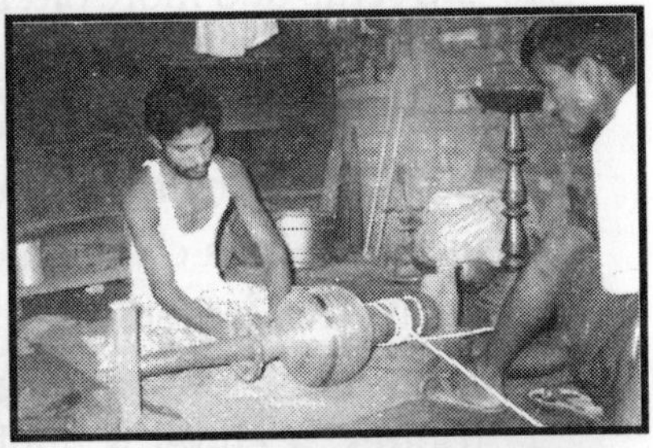

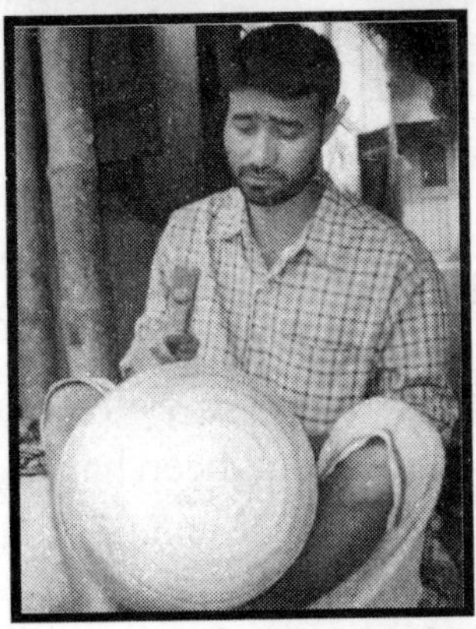

Brass Metal Worsk are at Progress at *Hajo*

technology of producing brass metal craft is being passed over for generations and the villagers take up these works as a tradition. The cheap, good looking machine-made brass and bell metal works are posing stiff competition as far as marketability of these crafts are concerned. Thus a heavy exodus of skilled craftsmen from this traditional work is seen in recent years.

- *Production process*: The raw materials obtained either through melting minerals or sometimes by melting old scrap and more often through sheet metal in the form of alloy of zinc and copper. At first the sheet metal are cut into several pieces as per measurement of the craft being produced. The pieces are burnt and melted in coal flame. Big hammers are used for giving the desired shape. The lathe machine is used sometimes for bending the sheets. As the lathe rotates, a chisel is applied to the part to get the required shape. Soldering of different parts is done by using a metal alloy which is prepared by the artisan himself. Polishing is done by vigorous rubbing either by hand or by feet, using a rug.

SARTHEBARI (A BELL METAL VILLAGE)

Sarthebari is well known for its bell metal works. Bell metal works need skill and training. The industry has been handed down within a few clans of a caste called "*Kanhar*". It is estimated that up to hundred tons of products are manufactured every year in Sarthebari, where almost 300 production units are working, each of which consists of 5 to 6 workers. The normal products of bell metal are the traditional plates, cups, tumblers, pitchers, bowls, *sarai*, dwarf pitchers, pots and musical instruments. The products are very popular inside the state as well as in neighbouring countries like Bhutan, Tibet and Nepal.

Fresh raw materials come in the form of *la* or tin and copper in the proportion of 83 per cent and 17 per cent respectively. These materials are procured from Muradabad (a famous place itself for bell metal works in Uttar Pradesh), Kolkata and Delhi. Scraps are also used in large proportion as the raw materials and this ensures recycling of the old and damaged materials.

- *Location*: Sarthebari is located in Barpeta district of Assam at a distance of 83 km (by Amingaon—Hajo Road) from Guwahati. Regular bus service is available between Guwahati and Sarthebari. Bus charges Rs. 35.00 and takes almost 3 hours from Guwahati. Taxi services are also available. Taxi charges Rs. 1000.00 from Guwahati for dropping at Sarthebari.
- *Manufacturing process*: Copper and tin are melted in a coal furnace and the resultant mixture is weighed in different trays called dices as per required measurement for the particular item. The required shape is given manually using hammers. The metal is immediately cooled down to room temperature by dipping it in water to make it tough and durable. Polishing is done by vigorous rubbing by hand using a rug like that of brass metal work.

NALBARI (A BAMBOO CRAFT VILLAGE)

Nalbari is a backward district of lower Assam just 65 km North West from Guwahati. The density of population of Nalbari is the highest among the districts dominated by indigenous people. The tradition of craft in this district is century old practice. The rural areas have been agog with the sounds of the looms. The weaving is dominated by the womenfolk as in many other areas of the State. However, the men are adept in fine bamboo crafts. The specialty of the entire district is the *Japi*. *Japi* is a traditional headgear of the rural community of Assam. Specially like in all South East Asian countries bamboo and wild grass with flat leaves have been crafted as a headgear for the cultivators for protection from sun and rain. However, in Assam it has special importance as a glamorous *purda* used during Ahom rules by the womenfolk of the kingdom as well as those of the affluent class. For this purpose the *japi* would be crafted at a bigger size so that it can hide the whole body of one woman. From then onwards the *japis* are attracting beautiful designs and now-a-days many colours with ornaments are used to make decorated *japi*. The decorative *japis* are not only very popular in Assam, the same has been embraced by many art lovers all over the country. Some very famous villages where *japi* is being produced almost in every household are Balamugkuchi, Japarkuchi, Sutarkuchi, Terecia and Digheli. All the villages are adjacent to each other and within a radius of 4 km from Nalbari town.

Photo Plate 3: Bamboo and Cane Works

The district is also famous for Erhee works. Many villages traditionally engage in rearing Erhee cocoons, spinning and then weaving beautiful warm scarves. Given the fact that Erhee textiles are expensive, the women of these villages can earn a handsome amount by selling them. However, with increase in alterative sources of income, this traditional art has not attracted new generations and thus it is feared that in the next few generations the weaving of Erhee scarves would no longer be found here. Some villages in the vicinity of Nalbari town which still practice the art of Erhee cultivation and weaving are Gandhiya, Belsar, Kakaya, Barnibari, Kaithalkuchi, Jowardi, Sahpur, Simalia, Bahjani and Solmari. All of them are within a distance of 15 km from Nalbari town and can be visited within a day or two.

BARPETA (AN ORNAMENTS OF IVORY VILLAGE)

- *Crafts and the local people*: Barpeta is famous for wonderful Assamese traditional ornaments of ivory. Its ivory works and cane and bamboo crafts bear distinctive mark of excellence in exquisite design and exclusive quality.
- Barpeta's ivory work is unique in the entire state, which is endemic to Barpeta only. Apart from traditional ornaments some other utility items like comb, fancy items were also made from ivory. However, the raw materials for this craft being ivory, became scarce as hunting of elephants has become

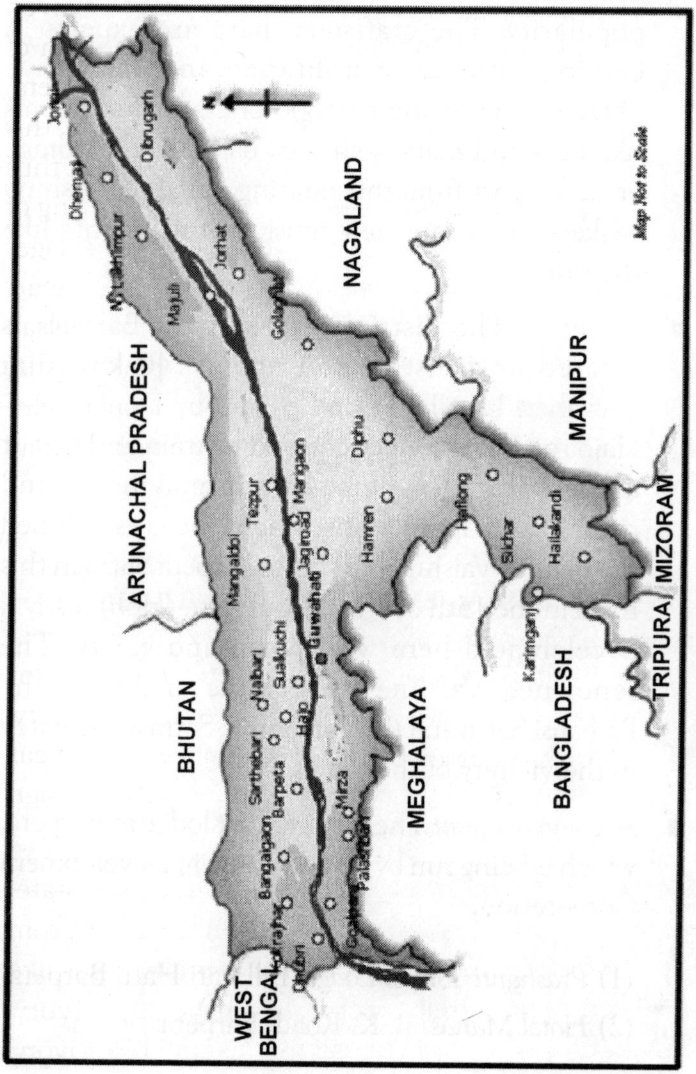

Map 3: Assam—Places of Craft Interest.

illegal for quite sometime now.

Barpeta's cane and bamboo crafts are now gaining popularity. The craftsmen here are experts in carving varieties of utilitarian and decorative objects. The exotic bamboo crafts include items like pots and mats, sofa sets, baskets and storage vessels, apart from the amazing range of finishing baskets, trays, and few musical instruments like the flute.

- *Location*: The district headquarters Barpeta is located at a distance of about 140 km from Guwahati by NH 31 and 84 km by Doulashal—Hajo road. It is well connected by train and bus. It is the traditional home of Vaishnavite art and culture. Mahapurush Shri Madhabdeva established the famous Vaishnavite shrine Barpeta Satra in this town in the 15th century. Doul Jatra (Holi) festival is celebrated here with pomp and gaiety. The renowned Vaishnavite Temple of Assam the Patbausi Satra and the Sundaridia Satra are situated in the vicinity of the town.
- *Accommodation*: There is a tourist lodge at Barpeta, which is being run by Assam Tourism Development Corporation.

  (1) *Prashanti Tourist Lodge*, Billatari Hati, Barpeta

  (2) *Hotel Manas*, B. K. Road, Barpeta

KOKRAJHAR

Kokrajhar is the Headquarter of Bodoland Territorial Council (BTC). BTC is predominantly inhabited by colourful people of the Bodo tribe, rich in folk dance and music. Spinning and weaving is the way of life of the Bodo people. The Bodos are famous for its colourful hand made textiles and Erhee scarves (kind of warm cloth made of natural fabric called Erhee or *Endi*). Kokrajar is well connected by bus and train.

- *Accommodation:* Some decent lodging facilities are available in the town. They are shown in the following table.

  Lodging Facilities at Kokrajhar

  - Bwirathi Lodge, R. N. B. Road
  - Monalisha Lodge, R. N. B. Road
  - Sahara Lodge, R. N. B. Road
  - OmShree Hotel, Near Petrol Pump (Assam Oil) with A/C. Room

- *Craft and local people*: Weaving is an integral part of the lives of all communities living in the Bodoland Territorial Council, specially in the district of Kokrajhar. It is a tradition of the region like that of whole of Assam and can be traced back to ancient period. Handloom is the major craft of Bodo people. The Bodo's are renowned for their rich heritage of weaving and Bodo women have

Photo Plate 4: Tribal Dresses

Karbi Traditional Dresses

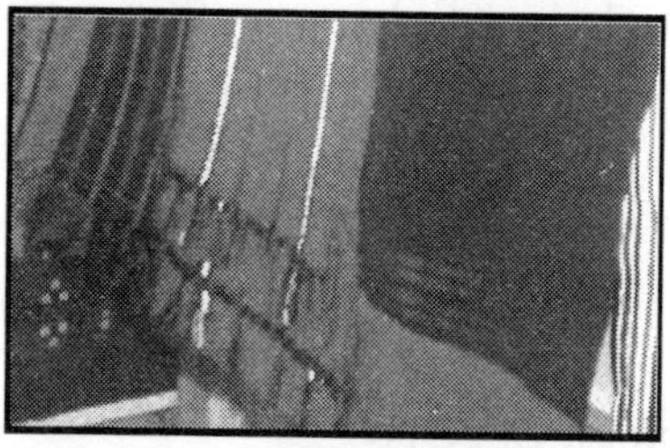

Dimasa Dresses

Karbi Scarves and Cloth Bag

Waist Coat with Bodo Design

been acknowledged as the finest weavers in the North East. They weave different types of cloths like—*Dakhna, Jumgra, Arnai* and also Muga and Erhee. The Bodo women use their traditional colours (bright yellow, orange and red in particular) in the Dakhna, a length of fabric which covers her from chest to foot, the Dakhna is a harmonious arrangement of *Asin Guddam* (bottom). Its elaborate borders distinguish it from the Assamese Mekhala with a variation of the strong bold strips and predominance of black and white punctuated by a smattering of green and yellow.

The Bodo people also weave export quality of Erhee (*Endee*) and Muga products. There are about 150 handloom production units with about 5,000 commercial weavers at Kokrajhar town area.

Saljora (A Bodo Village)

Saljora is only 1½ km from Kajol gaon, the District Head Quarters of newly formed Chirang District in the lower Assam. This village is only 8 km west of Bongaigaon town. All the 63 households of this village are proud owners of traditional looms. The looms meet the local demand and sometimes the surplus produces could be sold too. Traditional and most frequently woven dresses in Saljora are *Dakhna, Urnna and Gamusa.*

Photo Plate 5: Bodo Textile

A Bodo Woman in her Loom

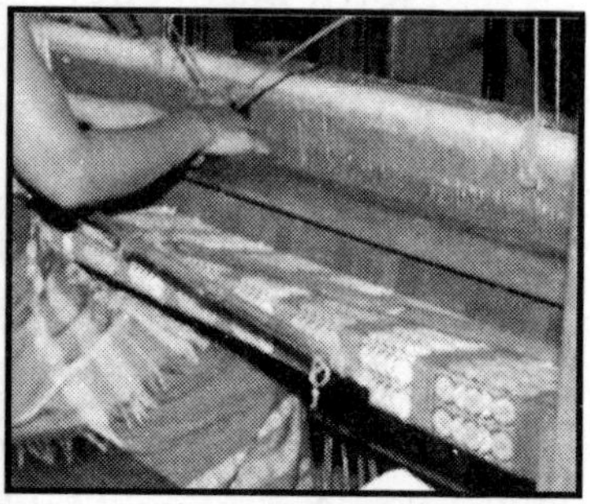

A *Dokhna* is being Woven by Bodo Damsel

Bodo Women Selling Traditional Textile

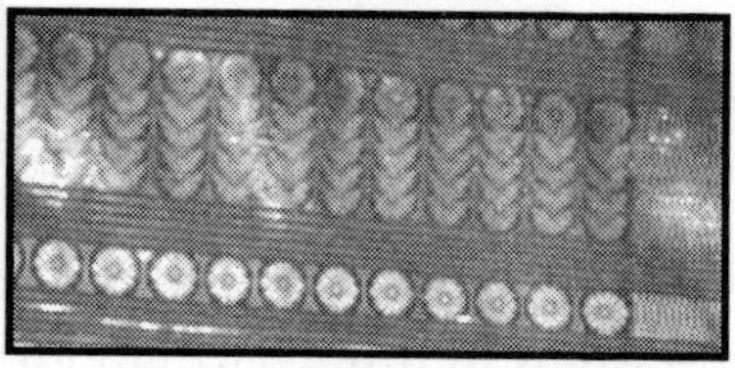

A Flowery Bodo Design

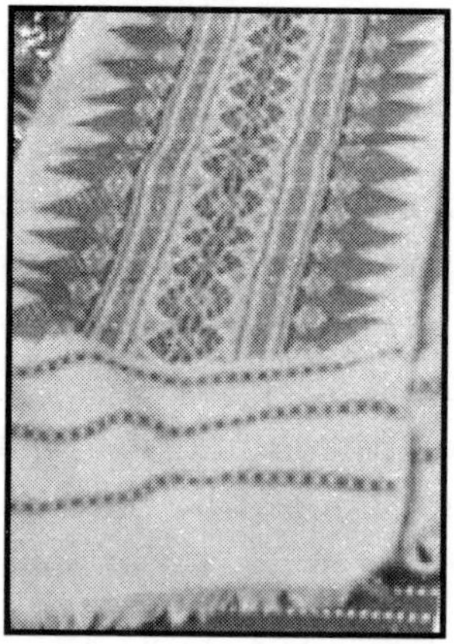

An *Arnal*

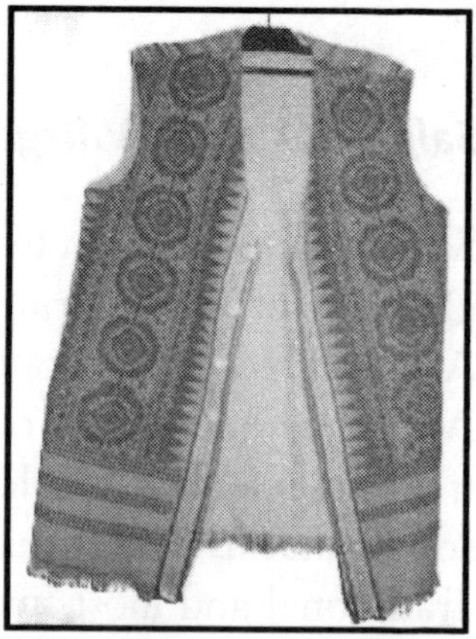

A Commercialised Bodo Design in a Jacket

Ambari

Ambari is a Bodo village situated at the international border with Bhutan, which is about 63 km. from Kokrajhar town. It is about 40 km. from the National Highway 31 by Bongaigaon Samtabari Road. This particular village is well known for its colourful culture and weaving. All local people of this village are expert in weaving. Like almost all Bodo and Assamese villages, each of the 93 households of this village owns a loom.

The craft villages may be visited with overnight accommodation at the nearest town of Bangaigaon. One can board at the Maharaj Hotel, Station Road, Old Bongaigaon or at Kanishka Hotel, Station Road, Old Bongaingaon or at Hotel Jahnaby, Near DC Bungalow, Bangaigaon.

ASHARIKANDI (A TERRACOTTA VILLAGE)

Asharikandi is situated on the North Bank of the Brahmaputra, in Dhubri District. It is 16 Km from Dhubri Town and only 4 km from Gauripur. Private Buses charge a fare of Rs. 8.00 from Dhubri Town. And only about 1 km south of N.H.-31.

- *Craft and the local people*: Asharikandi is a traditional village and it is well known for its pottery and terracotta works. Traditionally Asharikandi has been known for its pottery works. But for quite

Photo Plate 6: Looms

Korkrajhar

Sualkuchi

Ordinary Loom

sometimes now it is gaining popularity for its beautiful crafts in the form of terracotta. This terracotta industry has given unique identity to this village. There are a total of 80 families and all the households are engaged in terracotta and pottery craft.

The raw materials are transported through boats and the clay costs about Rs. 500.00 per boat (1200 kg). The average proceed of the finish product is about. 5,000.00 per month for a family.

- *Production process*: At first the clay that was collected by boat from the riverside is made smooth by adding water and 20 per cent sand. This mixture of clay, water and sand is kept away from direct sunlight and wind. The required shapes are given by free hand, and sometimes when repetitive figures are needed to be produced, some kind of dices are used. Then the shaped pieces are dried in sunlight. After colouring these items they are burnt at the temperature ranged between 100°C and 800°C.

Pottery items are made by potter's wheel. The objects are roughly shaped on the wheel at the beginning, then finished by beating the outside with a flat wooden beater and mushroom shaped stone block held inside the object. This process continues till the object reaches the required shape and desired thickness. The wheel is the common kind, thick with short spokes turning on a pivot of hard wood or metal, provided with a large hub acting as a revolving table. The impulsion is given by hand with a vertical stick inserted in a hole in the rim. The potter throws the painstakingly kneaded clay into the center of the wheel, rounding it of and then spinning the wheel around. As the whirling gathers momentum, he begins to shape the clay into the desired form. When finished he severs the shaped clay from the rest of the clay skillfully with a string.

The firing is mostly done in the open improvised kilns within a simple hollowed circular area, with the articles pilled up and covered by cow-dung cakes or the cheapest available fuel like rice husks and wood sands.

GAURIPUR (A SOLAPITH VILLAGE)

Gauripur, a small rural town is situated on the north bank of the Brahamaputra, in Dhuburi District of lower Assam. Gauripur is only 12 km east of Dhuburi town. It was the seat of the former Zamidar of Gauripur since 1850. The Raj family, as it is known in Gauripur, has contributed a great deal for promotion of art and culture in that region. The legend of Indian cinema, Pramothesh Ch. Baruah, the accomplished folk artist Pratima (Baruah) Pandey and wild life activist (known as the queen of elephant) Parbati Baruah, all belong to this famous family of Gauripur. Gauripur is well connected by Rail and Road.

- *Craft and the local people:* Gauripur and its adjoining area are well known for Sola-pith craft, popularly known as *Kuhila* craft. *Kuhila* craft is predominately practiced by the people from the Malakar

Photo Plate 7: Solapith Works

The Harvested Solapith Plants

Finished Solapith Works

community of the Gauripur area. The Sola-pith cluster of Japusabari, is famous for its craft works. The artisans here have been able to improve their living standard after joining hands as a cluster. The traditional skill of the predecessors handed over to the next generations has kept the awesome craft's traditional richness alive in spite of its limited reach. In greater Gauripur area houses about 85 families are still working on *Kuhila* Craft. Many of them use this craft as a medium of extra income beyond their primary livelihood.

A craft family can earn up to Rs. 2000.00 to Rs. 3500.00 per month by working this *Kuhila* product. A small family can run by this industry smoothly.

- *Raw materials*: The raw material for this craft is procured naturally from the plant sola, which belongs to the plant group of Dicotylendonous. Sola plants have spongy cellular tissues in its stems and branches. Sola plants can be cultivated in low land with abundant water. The tissues are extracted from the stems and branches after the same are dried in the sun.
- *Production process:* The spongy fibers of Sola plants are shaped and curved using very sophisticated hand held tools like knifes, and then necessary parts are joined together using a special type of adhesive that is made locally. Generally no external colours are used in traditional items.

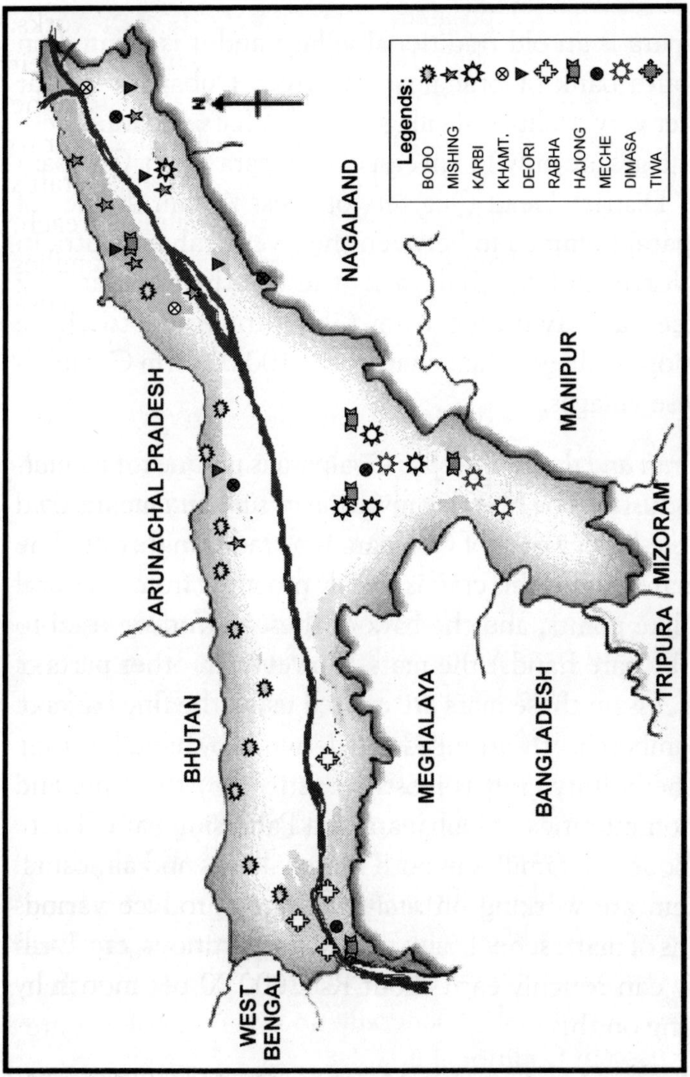

Map 4: Assam—Craft (Other than Textile) Producing Regions

DUBAPARA, GOALPARA

Dubapara is an old traditional village and it is located on the south bank of Brahamaputra river. Dubapara is near another very traditional village called Paharsingpara. These two villages are only 12 km east of Golapara Town. Goalpara is the District Head Quarters of West Assam district of Goalpara, hemmed in between the river Brahamaputra in the North and Meghalaya in the South. Regular taxi services are available from Goalpara town to these traditional villages. Taxi charges Rs. 100.00 form Goalpara to these villages.

Craft and the local people: Goalpara is unique for its *sital-pati* industry. The literal translation of *sital-pati* means cold mat. *Sital-pati* works of Goalpara is a traditional craft. The raw materials for this craft is mainly procured from a natural grass like plants, and the bark of these plants are used to knit (by bare hands) the mats. However, in other parts of lower Assam these mats are crafted using the fine barks of the bamboo neatly arranged and designed by hand knitting. This hereditary craft is mostly practiced by the *Nadi* and *Dey* communities of Dubapara and Paharsing para. There are about 180 families in both these villages and almost all of them are working on *sital-pati.* They produce various designs of mats, school bags, tablemats, partitions, etc. Each family can roughly earn about Rs. 2000.00 per month by working on this.

One can have comfortable stay in Goalpara in privately run hotels and in the Government Circuit House. The

Photo Plate 8: Sital Pati

Improvised Sital Pati Products: (*Clock-wise from top left*) Bags, Ladies Purses, Fruit Basket etc.

A Common Design of Sital Pati

A Craftswoman Busy Knitting Sital Pati at Bubapara Goalpara

hotels are Hotel Siddharth, Pancharatna Road, Hotel Blue Diamond, Pancharatna Road and Hotel Hollywood, Main Road.

KARBI ANGLONG

Although this colourful Hills district is dominated by the Karbi population it is the home of many other tribes and non-tribes like Bodo-Cachari, Dimasa, Mech, Naga, Kuki and Nepali, Assamese and Bengali. The Karbis are rich in handicrafts and weaving. They have significant number of designs of traditional dresses and have been using hand made utensils from very ancient time. The district Head Quarters are in Diphu, some 270 km away from Guwahati by road. Diphu is connected by railways too.

'*Jambiliathan*' (a tree having many branches with hornbills) is a remarkably unique Karbi craft made of woodcarving. Availability of raw materials (like cane, bamboo, wood, etc.) have made it easier for the local artisans to engage in mind boggling creative works. These works mainly include basketry, utensils, musical instruments, and decorated furniture not only for household use but also for interior decoration. They are also experts in making typical houses with cane, bamboo and wood. The handlooms are also another important aspect of Karbi day-to-day life. The women folk are mostly engaged in weaving of Pini, *Pekok*, turban, and scarf, etc. Some villages which are significant in craft tradition are described below.

Photo Plate 9: Few Crafts from Karbi Anglong

Hak: Karbi Bamboo Storage Devices

Dry Flowres Produced in *Karbi Anglong*

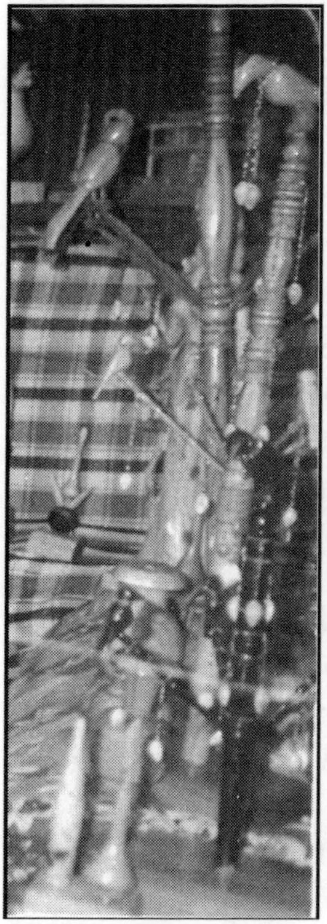

Jamila Than: Scared Woodcarving of the Karbis

Hingru: Karbi Bamboo Rice Beer Filtering Device

Hamren

Hamren is treated as the capital of Karbi traditional life. It is rich in Karbi crafts and culture. Wood carving, cane and bamboo works, blacksmithy are still practiced in and around Hamren. Langtupthepi, Phongjungre, Kongseck, Langsude, Chandrapur, Rongkhang Rongbo (Rong Arak), Hamthor, Phonkrei are some important villages in the vicinity of Hamren.

Boithalangsu

Biothalangsu is also an important area for crafts especially traditional looms and Cane and Bamboo works. Some villages where craftsmanship is still flourishing are Umru, Longri, Rongkarlasu, Khong, Dongka, Menmeji and Pungahidi:

- *Kherani* famous for jute works, mat making, rope making and cane and bamboo works.
- *Bokajan* is famous for cane and bamboo works (for both household and decorative), wood carving and looms.
- *Manja* is a very famous for pottery and wood carving
- *Dhanshiree Valley* is famous for Dimasa traditional crafts.
- *Dictotgaon* is famous for bamboo and cane works
- *Dengaon* is located adjacent to Nagaon District of and Assam, is famous for Wood carving

Some Significant Traditional Crafts of Karbi Anglong

- *Traditional Dress*: *Pekok* (cloth for covering the lower portion of woman's body), *Pini* (cloth for upper portion of women), *Pecharpi* (Scarf), Jackets, *Poho* (headgear for men), muffler and *Venkok* (textile waist band for women). In fact, the Karbi Jackets are gaining popularity among urban dwellers in recent times in the plains also.
- *Handloom Instruments*: Harpi (Dopodi), Thenging, Baptheli.
- *Musical Instruments*: Cengbaruk, Kundengdong, Kumliang,
- *Household items*: *Tibuk* (pot), *Horbong* (wooden pot to keep traditional rice beer), *Harluk, Tob* (kind of tub made by cane, bamboo and wood), *Seru* (wooden kettle), *Hatan* (baskets made of bamboo and cane), *Hak* (basket that's being carried on the solder with a strap on the head to carry goods and fire wood), *Bora* (beautiful cane box use to keep cloths), *Murjong* (cane made basket to keep rice), *Khangra* (basket used for carrying wood), *Hingru* (filter made of bamboo used while making rice beer), *Chignam* (very significant strap made of cane used to carry basket, *Lumphuk* (wooden rice spoon of bigger size), *Beleng* (bamboo tray), *Hangkrung* (bamboo filter to sort mainly rice), *Tar* (stiff mat made of bamboo).

NORTH CACHAR (NC) HILLS

NC Hills is one of the two hill districts of Assam situated in the Borail range. It is located 92 39' to 93 37" E Longitude and 25 30" to 25 47"N Latitude with an area of 4890 sq km and at an altitude from 600m to 1866 m. The temperature hovers around 24 to 26 Celsius and average rainfall is 246 ml per year. According to 2001 census it has a population of 1,86,189 from two subdivisions of Haflong and Maibong. There are 4 towns and 640 villages under 5 development blocks—Harangajao, Diyung Mukh Valley, Jatinga Valley, Diyungbra and Sabar. The administration in the hill district is run by an autonomous council known as NC Hills Autonomous District Council. Haflong is the district headquarters. It is 240 km. from Shillong, 112km. from Silchar, 261 km. from Nagaon, 350 km. from Guwahati and 214 km from Dimapur (in Nagaland) by road. One can have comfortable stay at Hotel Elite, Hotel Joyeswary or at the beautiful Circuit House overlooking the Lumding-Silchar railway line crisscrossing the not so distant hill ranges.

Although it is popularly known as land of Dimasa the dwelling is shared among 13 tribes—Zeme, Kuki, Khasi, Hmar, Biate, Chakma, Lusai, Karbi, Hrangkhol, Vaiphai, Thadou, Syntengs/Pnar and Khelma. Some non tribals are also found to have permanent residence in NC hills and prominent among them is Bengali speaking Muslim population.

The N.C. Hills are rich in crafts. During the time of

Ahom rule the then Dimasa King established his kingdom in Dimapur first and later shifted its base to Maibong in NC hills. As a Royal community Dimasa had an old tradition of craftsmanship. The Khaspur, Dimapur and Maibong ruins are the evidence of their artistic mind. Other tribes also got the opportunity of developing their artistic crafts under the Dimasa kingdom and thus whole hill region is found to have tremendously rich heritage of craftsmanship. Using the easily available raw materials in the rich jungles of the hills the people craft varieties of baskets (locally known as *Lonkrai*), Mats, boxes (*Khailung*), furniture, utensils and other decorative items from wood, cane and bamboo for their day-to-day use and also for interior decoration of private residences and public halls. Their expertise in bamboo and cane works can be established by the typically designed houses in the villages. On the other hand, the womenfolk weave cloths using the craftsmanship gifted by generations of knowledge in weaving. Most women know and are practically engaged with weaving designs which are highly appreciated. Marriageable girls weave their own bridal apparels by themselves. The colours used by them for dyeing yarns are prepared from raw indigo and wild herbs. They are also experts in spinning. Now a days the weaving and manufacturing of bamboo and cane products are two important cottage industries of NC Hills.

Every tribe has its unique craft distinguished in terms of design, motifs and manufacturing techniques. The traditional dress of Dimasa differs from Hmar or Khasi people in terms of wearing and weaving. The Dimasa Erhee scarves and other hand-woven items are very beautiful and highly demanded in the urban market. The tradition of carpentry among the Dimasa men is still alive and flourishing. The Dimasa hat and baskets are some of the remarkable cane crafts found in this region. The Hmars and Kukis are experts in carpentry, particularly in household items. The Zemes and Khasis are expert in cane and bamboo works and also in weaving. The Bengali speaking people of Harangajao area make beautiful cane furniture. With the help of DRDA (District Rural Development Agency, a State Government Agency) Self-help Groups (SHGs) among different tribes run commercial selling counters in the market area of Haflong Town for promotion of their craft works.

Some important villages or regions of NC Hills for crafts are described below:

Dimasa Dominated Areas

- *Longma* is an important Dimasa Village near Haflong.
- *Sontila* is 13 km from Haflong town famous for Dimasa craft.
- *Sarkari Bagan* is located in Lower Haflong just 6 km from Haflong town. It is also famous for craft works.
- *Gunjung* is an important Dimasa village in Shillong Road just 30 km from Haflong.

- *Dehangi* is another important Dimasa dominated area in Shillong Road. It is at a distance of 50 km from Haflong.

Some remarkable craft producing areas around Maibong, which is 53 km away from Haflong are Thanalambra (38 km from Haflong famous for Dimasa Crafts), Thaijuwari, Guruwari, Khemphaidisa, Lambadisa, Khebre, Khejurband and Gaetahaja.

Hmar Dominated Area

As mentioned above Hmar is a very important tribe of the NC hills district. The hmars can boast of rich and unique culture and thus special craft works. *Maoloy Basti* a Hmar village in Haflong—Shillong Road is situated at a distance of 4 km from Haflong. It is famous for woodcraft. The craftsmen make decorative items, TV stand, Astray, Candle stand, bed, table, chair (all from wood), etc.

- *Redjil* is a Hmar village of Haflong and famous for traditional dress, Harangajao is 46 km from Haflong and is famous for cane and bamboo crafts. Toulpui and Sangmar are also famous for textiles besides cane and bamboo works.
- *Tingpui* and *Diyun* are two prominent Baite villages of NC hills famous for their rich textile works
- *Jatinga* is just 8 km from Haflong town near the Borail range and rich in Khasi traditional craft works.

- *Longkok* is located in Lower Haflong and is an important Hrangkhol dominated area.

The rich craft tradition of Zemes could be found in Bora Haflong (5 km from Haflong town), Laisung (6 km from Haflong), Lodi, Bagita, Bauringlai, Mikibari and Kubin (all situated at a radius of 10 km from Halflong).

Kuki traditional crafts can be witnessed in the villages of Rose Rope (about 30 km from Halflong in Halflong Maibong road) and Sumpijung (near Maibong).

Mahur is famous for its textile work, which is dominated by Manipuri community.

Some Significant Crafts of Dimasas

Cane, bamboo and wood crafts: *Longkrai* (cane made basket used to carry fire wood), *Khagkra* (big basket made by both cane and bamboo for keeping goods), *Jengkra* (a beautiful basket made by both cane and bamboo for keeping cloths), *Khailung* (wooden box used for keeping cloths and valuable objects like ornaments), *Khamplu* (basket made by both cane and bamboo for storing rice), *Tupi* (cane hat), *Changkrong* (flat bamboo tray), *Samtu* (wooden grinder), *Intui* (bamboo basket), *Insung* (big wooden box for storing cloths and ornaments), *Kang* (small bamboo basket), *Kungbung* (medium sized bamboo basket), *Indrew* (like *Changkrong*), *Ingui* (bamboo stiff mat), *Tukjung* and *Kapaijung* (bamboo filter).

Textile: *Rigu* (women's cloth for lower portion), *Remai* (wrapper) and *Rekhausa Rimi* (woman's cloth for upper portion)

Longkhai—a beautiful cane basket of Khasi mostly used for carrying goods.

Some traditional textile items found among **Bishnupriya** community of NC hills are *Khou* (bag), *Matha* (bedspread), *Khulei* (towel), *Enapi* (for woman's upper part), *Tulphui* and *Angului* (for lower part).

Some Zeme traditional crafts are *Terota, Discoraji Sanjoyraji, Ntui* (box), *Longkai* (cone shaped basket), *UngKa* (Basket), *Nrau* (bamboo tray) and *Krau* (basket type bamboo filter).

MAJULI

A vibrant tradition of art and craft is an important component of the collage of Majuli, which is priceless. This includes handlooms, basketry, pottery, wood carving, mask-making, ivory-work, silver-filigree work, cane and bamboo work, mat-making (Googol-work, Patidoi work, Banana stream works) and boat making; these are some of the traditional crafts still being carried on in this wonderful river island.

Majuli, considered as "the largest" fresh-water inhabited river island of the world situated in the midst of the river Brahmaputra, is a civil subdivision of Jorhat District in upper

Photo Plate 10: Few Crafts of Majuli

Traditional Bamboo and Paper Mask of Majuli

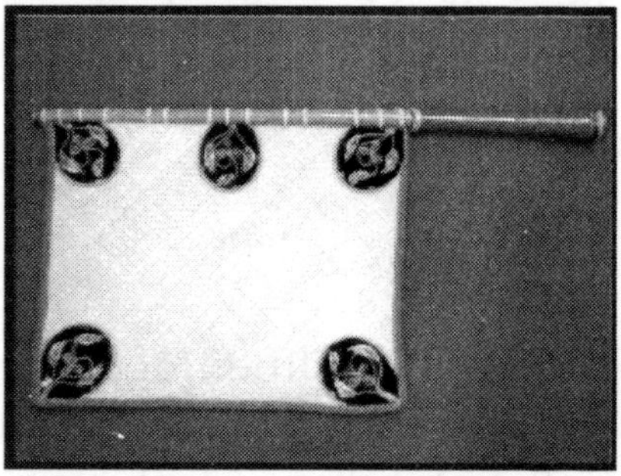

Traditional Hand Fan

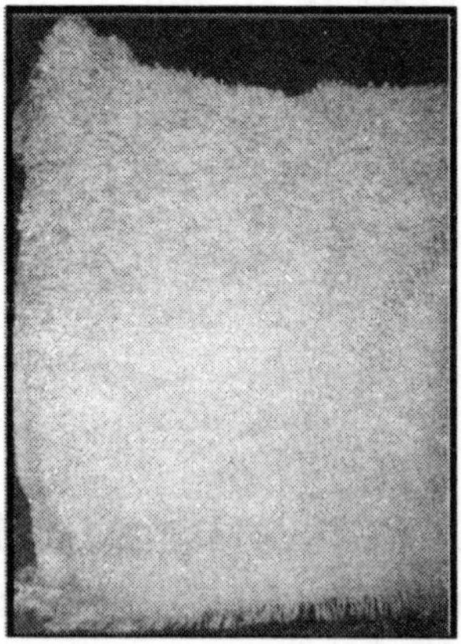

Mirijim

Assam. This 886sq km land mass is known as centre of the Vaishnavite art and culture. The *Sattras*, which are the primary institution of Vaishnavite faith, have been playing an important role in making craft work a tradition and custom of the region. There are 22 such *Sattras* found in Majuli. In and around the *Sattras* there are 243 villages, inhabited by different communities. In all these villages majority of the population is acquainted with one or the other craftwork. The common artifacts include hand woven textiles manufactured either by using waist held looms or by framed ones, basketry, and various tools for fishing made of bamboo.

- *Location:* Majuli is situated in the midst of river Brahmaputra in the district of Jorhat and can be reached by steamers only. It is convenient to cross the river from southern bank, as the river is narrower this side. However, steamer service is available from the northern bank too. One can take the steamer from Nimati Ghat at the southern bank which is 12 km from Jorhat town. The steamer charges Rs. 15.00 per person, Rs 20.00 for each two-wheeler and Rs. 350.00 for light vehicle. Kamalabari is treated as the central point of the entire island for its easy connectivity from Jorhat town through steamers. The steamers take longer time during the winter months as the riverbed becomes shallow and thus has to take a longer route. The average time taken (from Nimati Ghat to Kamalabari) is about 90 minutes. The southern port of Nimati Ghat is well connected to Jorhat by road. Regular and comfortable public transportation services like bus is available to and from Jorhat.

- *Accommodation at Majuli*: Decent guest house accommodation is available at Na Sattra, South Kmalabari *Sattra*, Kamalabari, Majuli. Almost all *Sattras* are having facility for accommodating guests.

During the Ahom rule Majuli had some professionals engaged in working with crafts like *Pati* (Mat) at Potiya Gaon, *Kohal* at Kohal Gaon, *kamar* (blacksmithy) at Kamar Gaon, *Kumar* (pottery) at Salmora, *Tanti* (weaver) and *Jogi and Nath* (rearing silkworm) at Ratanpur and Phulani area. However, *Barhois* (cane and bamboo workers) could be found in every village. The tradition is still practiced by majority of the populace in these villages even after many generations. The availability of raw materials like Bamboo, Cane, Wood, herbs like Googol plants, Banana steams, and steams of *Patidoi* too help the artisans to stick to these works. Almost all musical instruments apparently essential for the *Nam Prasang*—a daily ritual of the *Sattras* and other Vaishnavite shrines like *Namghars*—the *Taal, Khol, Daba, Sangkha*, and those are needed for folk songs and dances, for which too Majuli is famous for *Dhol, Taka, Sutuli, Pepa* etc. are all made by local artisans. Moreover, different utility products used in daily lives of the people of Majuli like the utensils are made by these artisans. Few articles of daily life crafted using gold, silver, bell-metals are preserved in *Sattra* museum. Few of them are *Ban Kahi*, *Ban bati*, *Sarai*, *Bor*

Sarai, *Gong* (all made of brass), Decorative enameled Knives, inlaid work, Silver filigree, brass icon of Gods and Goddesses, silver tray with motifs of Krishna, ivory paduka, golden stick, ivory comb, can made fan, etc are important documents.

Some significant crafts of this area are discussed in detail in the following paragraphs.

Wood Carving

Wood Carving is one of the most attractive artifacts of Majuli. Decorated pieces for the front door of the every quarter of the *Sattra*, the mask of Gods and Goddess, animals which depict the walls of the *Sattras* or *Namaghars*, religious utensils like *Xarai*, *Bota* (for offering betel nut for the honoured guests in religious gatherings or at households), *Thoga* (for keeping religious books, wherefrom the reader reads in the form of religious songs) are some important examples of excellent craftsmanship of the people of Majuli. However, the craftsmen of the present day have chosen to be a little commercial in order to earn their livelihood and shifted their attention to decorative items (like the models of Majuli itself, and locally available birds and animals) made of wood carvings. Another remarkable craftsmanship of the State, which is abundantly found among the craftsmen of Majuli is the wooden boxes made for household uses. Some of these are known as *Bora-pera*, *Hatani-pera*, and these are basically used for preserving cloths and valuable objects.

Manuscript Making

Another very important and glorious craft of the river island is manuscript making, which makes Majuli unique in the entire India and east Asia. In the ancient times, before the discovery and mass use of common paper the religions leaders of the *Sattras* wrote manuscripts on the papers made from the bark of the Plant *Sanchi* using traditional natural ink prepared from the *Keheraj* stems and coloured it by natural colourants like *Hengul* and *Haital*. The *Hosti Vidyarnava*—a pictorial manuscript on elephant keeping is still preserved in *Auniati Sattra*. There are a good number of manuscripts still preserved in different *Sattras*. This practice and art of manuscript making is still preserved by a jealous group of very gifted craftsmen.

Mask Making

It is a unique traditional art, which is available only in Majuli in the state of Assam. The masks in Majuli are used primarily during the enactment of religious stories in the form of *bhawona* or drama in the Vaishnavait institutions. Traditional mask making is seen in Sikkim and also in some parts of Arunachal Pradesh. The uniqueness of Majuli lies in the fact that the masks are made of bamboo with the combination of paper and cloth unlike those of Arunachal Pradesh where they are primarily made of wood carving. This combination of bamboo, paper and cloth make it lightweight so that the actors can easily carry the burden. Different types of masks are seen in Majuli—small and big, replica of Gods and Goddesses, demons, birds, animals, etc. Sometimes they cover only the mouth of the actor (*Mukh-mukha*) or whole mouth (*Suti-mukha* or *Lotokai Mukha*) or whole body (*Soo Mukha*). The artisans first make the skeleton with bamboo and then cover it with paper or cloth or a mixure of these two. The necessary shapes and contours are given by using mud. Finally the mask is coloured with traditional natural colourants (Hengul *and* Haital), natural blue, or other home made colours. Now a days the masks are used to decorate the walls of *Sattras* as well as the drawing rooms of the solicitors in the townships.

Pottery

Pottery is an age-old tradition of the Kumar community of Salmora village. The artisans are experts in making various kinds of pots (*Kalah, Tekeli, Vabuki, Mala, Nadiya* etc.). The modernized crafts include flowerpots, toys, earthen statues, etc.

Handloom

The handloom sector of Majuli retains a place of pride in Assam particularly for its *Mirizim* and Erhee (or Endee) shawls. *Mirizim* traditionally is the expertise of the Mishing community, whereas the Erhee rearing, spinning, and weaving can also be found in other lower Assam districts as well irrespective of community. Traditional dresses like *Mekhala-Chadar*, *Cheleng* and *Shawls* are

Photo Plate 11: Pottery

Pottery is being Produced by an Assamese Women in *Majuli*

Raw Pottery and Burning of many of them Together

Way to the Market for Pottery

produced in the looms of the weavers. The Mishing women are fond of weaving *Ribi Gaseng* (a cloth used by women at the upper portion of the body), *Mibu Galok* (stitched colourful cloth for the lower portion) apart from the *Mirizim*.

Bamboo and Cane Work

The artisans of Majuli are also experts in bamboo and cane works. They make different types of utilitarian baskets (like *Bor-pachi*, *Saru-pachi*, *Kharahi*, *Nichuka kharahi*, *Dala* etc.), household furniture (like beds, chair, table, *Murha* (stool made of finely knitted bamboo sticks, etc., fishing equipments (like *polo*, *jokai-Khaloi*, *caloni*, *Juluki*, *Sepa*, *Khoka*, *Ghani*, *Ubhati*, *Hukuma*, *Pocha*). Modernised crafts include among others some decorative items including items for interior decorations. However, these are *not* endemic to Majuli alone and can be found almost all over the state of Assam. The fans made of cane in the vicinity of Auniati and Kamalabari *Sattras* are remarkable pieces of craftsmanship.

Although all races or communities engaged in these traditional crafts the designs, motifs and manufacturing process of communities differ. For example, the Mishing's crafts like baskets, looms are different from Deories.

Sattras of Majuli

A very brief description of *Sattras* of Majuli with respect to richness in traditional crafts is offered below.

- Auniati *Sattra* is situated 5 km west of Kamalabari. This *Sattra* is famous for beautiful fan made of cane (as mentioned above), bamboo works and ancient manuscripts. The *Sattra* museum has preserved many traditional and ancient craft items.
- Natun Kamalabari *Sattra*—This *Sattra* is situated 1.5 km south of Kamalabari, famous for its cane and bamboo crafts.
- Uttar Kamalabari—Just 1.5 km north of Kamalabari, famous for its wood carvings apart from exquisite bamboo works.
- Garamurh *Sattra* is situated at the heart of the Garamurh township. It is famous for its woodcrafts and bamboo work settings decorated during Rasa festival
- Kerella Gaon—Situated just 1.5 km south of Garamurh and is famous for mask-making, bamboo *and* cane works.
- Adialengi *Sattra*—5 km west of Garamurh also famous for mask and bamboo works.
- Bengena Ati *Sattra*—4 km east of Kamalabari and famous for its museum where various old age utensils, manuscripts are preserved.
- Bhogpur *Sattra* is 6 km east of Kamalabari. One can witness beautiful murals and wall paintings, woodcarvings, crafting of Goolol mats, and Boat making in this *Sattra.*
- Bihimpur *Sattra*—9 km east of Kamalabari near Raonapar and is significant for blacksmith works
- Natun Samaguri—It is situated 10 km east of

Kamalabari and is well known for its Masks making tradition, bamboo works. The adjoining villages can be treated as an ideal craft villages.

- Purana Samaguri *Sattra*—3 km south of Bongaon and 17 km east of Kamalabari, famous for its mask making tradition.
- Narasimha *Sattra*—35 km east of Kamalabari near Jengrai; the *Sattra* is famous for its crafts like mask making and cane and bamboo works.
- Bahpholiya *Sattra*—Near to Narasimha *Sattra*, it is also centre of mask making and wood craft.
- Dakhinpat *Sattra*—This is one of the oldest *Sattras* of Majuli. Manuscripts making, mural paintings, wall paintings, woodcrafts, cane and bamboo works and googol mat making, are some significant craft works associated with these *Sattras*. It is situated 5 km south of Bongaon and 24 km from Kamalabari.

Some of the important villages from the point of view of craft works are mentioned below:

- *Solmara* is a land of pottery situated 20 km east of Kamalabari on the bank of the river Brahmaputra.
- *Sensowa* is a scheduled cast dominated area situated 10 km east of Kamalabari near Raonapar—very significant in fishing traps.
- *Jengrai* is dominated by the Mishing tribe and situated 15 km east of Garamurh, It is significant for Mishing looms and cane and bamboo crafts.
- *Srirampur* is a Deori village and enriched with looms and crafts. It is located near Jengrai.

Besides this Dhapak, Rangachahi, Saringiyati, Ratanpur, Gayan Gaon, Kamar Gaon, Majarbari, Khalihamari are some other villages famous for traditional craft works.

LAKHIMPUR

Lakhimpur is a District of East Assam, which is situated on the North bank of the Brahamaputra. The District is divided into two sub-divisions—North Lakhimpur and Dhakuakhana. Mishings and Bodos are the dominating tribes in this district. Apart from them a large number of caste Hindus speaking different languages (Assamese, Nepali etc.) are also living there for ages. The District Head Quarters, North Lakhimpur is the nerve center of trade and learning. The district is well known for the magical weaving of Mishing people. North Lakhimpur is well connected by Road and Rail. This town is also like a gateway to the Arunachal Pradesh.

Hotels of North Lakhimpur town are providing suitable accommodation to the visitors. The existing prominent lodging facilities are—

Lodging Facilities in Lakhimpur District

- Hotel Green View, Old R. M. S. Road;
- Asha Hotel, Near Public Bus Stand;
- Anupam Hotel, Super Market;

- Hotel Punjab, Near Public Bus Stand;
- Hotel Malinee, K. B. Road.

Main Craft and the Local People: Lakhimpur District is mostly inhabited by Mishing community. The Mishings are an important ethnic group of the larger Assamese populace in terms of numerical strength, socio-cultural traits, etc. The Mishings have a prominent characteristics—that they are used to wear self-woven cloth. Cultivation is prime occupation of the Mishings, and weaving has become a constant source of income for the women folk of the community.

One of the most common sounds one hears in a Mishing village is clack—clack of the loom that expresses the vibrating culture of the community. Mishing women have been acknowledged as one of the finest weavers, and marvelous designers. They reinvent their traditional diamond patterns in countless weaves. Their favourite colours are orange, yellow, green black and red. Their famous "*mirizim*" shawls and blankets make great bedspreads and even wall hangings too. Their main traditional product are—*Aga, Gasar, Garo, Mibu: Galuk, Ugom, Ri: bigasang, Yamba, Gapa, Dumer* (hand towel), *Erhi-Chadar* (scarf made of Erhi fiber), etc.

Different Types of Mishing Hand-Woven Textiles and their Design

The weaving industry of Mishing is related with their art,

Photo Plate 12: Mishing Diamond Designs

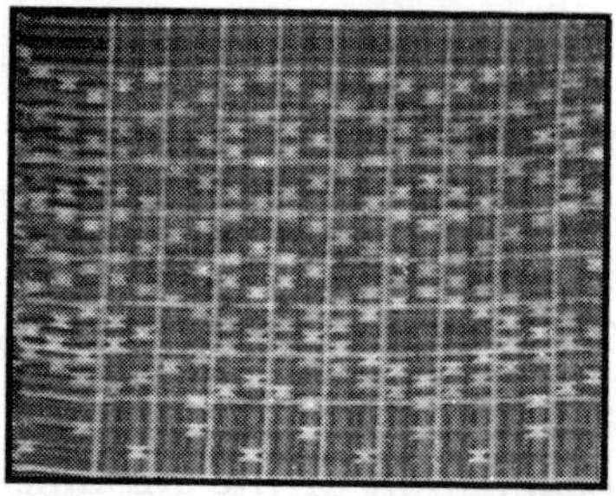

culture and tradition. In the weddings it is compulsory for the Mishings to wear self-woven clothes. The prominent characteristics of Mishing cloths are the colour combination, selection of motif and their unique design. They always give priority to bright colourful designs. They mainly design their clothes by different colour threads—orange, yellow, green, black and red. The designs consist of natural sceneries, group of flying birds, sprays of towers, star, tree and numerous combinations of geometrical patterns. They have maintained their traditional textile motifs of animals and also adopted designs and motifs from the neighbouring communities. This has added a new and magical lease of life to the very complexion of textiles. In their traditional clothes the design is usually in floral pattern, with animals like—deer, elephants inter-spread with lions, horses, leaves, birds and spring. Traditional motifs like fish, cons and crossed swords, etc. can also be found in Mishing textiles. Some motifs on white, black or other background colours make them very exotic. The bird motifs are red and white in colour and are triangular in shapes and rhythmically they follow a triangular formation. The design and colour combination of Mishing female garments are comparatively brighter and highly decorated than those of men. They have their own traditional natural techniques of colouring the designing threads. The women are adept in using simple handlooms for weaving their clothes.

Mirizim: *Mirizim* as mentioned above is the most important and exotic kind of shawl or blanket of the Mishing community. Weaving of *mirizim* is as a household tradition. As per custom the women of the community weave *mirizims* according to the number of their children, at least one for each child. *Mirizim* is a very august and precious wedding gift for the newly wed, and it is treated as the duty of the mother to do so with a self-woven blanket. The weaving process of *mirizim* is very complex and laborious. It is woven from completely raw cotton fabrics. Cotton fabric is said to be the pearl of Indian weaving. At first the cottonseeds are extracted from cotton and dried. Then the fine threads are spun out in form of thin cord. The fine threads are spun with hand spindles not in the spinning wheel. The weaving is done on the simple local loom. *Mirizim* is very long lasting blanket, which serves as a warm cover in many winters.

Mishing Traditional Villages

Here the location and tradition of a few Mishing villages are offered. These villages are chosen for the sheer convenience of location and accommodation so that the tourist can have a tour of these villages to witness the traditional weaving of the community in comfort.

Ghagar: Ghagar is a traditional Mishing village, which is situated by the Subansiri River, in Lakhimpur District. It is only 12 km Southeast from North Lakhimpur town. Taxi services are available on rent from North Lakhimpur town. Taxi charges Rs. 150.00 to Rs. 200.00 to drop at Ghagar. The number of households in the village is 65. Every house proudly possesses at least one local traditional loom under their Chang Ghar (house with elevated platform—the traditional housing style of the Mishings).

Photo Plate 13: Birth of the Golden Threads

Muga Silk Worm and the Cocoons with Resultant Golden Threads

Hand Spinning Machine

Automatic Spinning Machine

Ghunasuti: Another extraordinary village of the district is Ghunasuti, which is also known as "*Jonki-Panoi* village", named after a famous story of Jonki and Panoi. It is situated between the Brahamaputra and Subansiri rivers at a distance of about 16 km from the North Lakhimpur town. One has to cross the Subansiri by machine boat and has to walk about 4 km to reach the village. Ghunasuti is a big area and predominantly inhabited by the Mishings and very rich in art and culture. Weaving is their prime craft and they have always been using self-woven clothes. The women folk of the village are expert in making different types of Mishing traditional clothes like *Mirizim, Makhela Chaddor, Mibu, Galuk, Ribigasang,* Erhee *Chaddor, Gamucha* etc.

Tajik Gaon, Gogamukh: Tajik Gaon is 2.5 km from Gogamukh main center at Dhemaji District. Gogamukh is situated at a distance of 28 km from Dhemaji town. It is a Mishing ethnic village. There is a total of about 260 households in the village. The women and the young girls of this village are expert in weaving. They weave their household clothes like—*Mekhala—Chaddor, Gamucha, Mirizim, Mibu, Galuk, Ribigasang,* Erhee *Chaddor,* etc.

Accommodation at Gogamukh: After visiting the ethnic village visitors can accommodate themselves at Forest Guest House at Gogamukh; Akangshya Inn lodging, N. T. Road, Opposite Police Station, Gogamukh or at Jonmoni Restaurant and Lodge, Dhemaji Road, Gogamukh.

Pomuwa, Gogamukh: Pomuwa is a Mishing traditional village and is only 3 km away from Gogamukh Central. This traditional Mishing Village has two parts Ujani

Photo Plate 14: Snap-Shots

A Boat is being Carved

Modernized Dimasa Cane Works

A Dimasa Cane Hat, Wooden Grinder, and a Storage Device

Wooden Tea Pots and Spoons

Pamuwa and Namoni Pomuwa. The number of household is around 200 at present and as usual every house possesses its own loom locally made of bamboo and wood. The women and the young girls are expert in weaving different traditional clothes. The winner of State Tribal Handloom Designer Awards, 2004 belongs to this village. This particular traditional village is only 7 km away from Bordoibam—Beelmukh Birds' Sanctuary, It is on the way to Dhakuwakhana and is well connected by road.

Karichuk, Dhemaji: Karichuk is only 1.5 km away from Dhemaji Bus Station and only 1 km from Dhemaji Railway Station. Karichuk is in Dhemaji town area and is dominated by people from the Mishing community. There is a total about 300 Mishing families residing in this area. Even if their main livelihood is Government service, keeping up with tradition every house has at least one loom for meeting their own requirement of clothes. Now-a-days they have started weaving traditional clothes for commercial purpose also.

Tourists can board at any of these three prominent lodges available at Dhemaji. They are Raj Hotel, Main Road Dhemaji, Hotel Manash, Main Road Dhemaji and Shikha Hotel, Station Road, Dhemaji.

Bahir-Jonai, Jonai: Jonai civil Sub-Division is situated at the northeastern corner of Dhemaji District of Assam. Bahir-Jonai is only 4 km far away from Jonai Town, which is also dominated by the Mishings. They are very rich in their art and culture, particularly in weaving in the traditional loom. There are about 100 households in this village.

One can stay in Jonai at Jonai Circuit House; C. K. Hotel and Restaurant, Jonai Bazar or at Beauty Hotel, Near Railway Station.

Ratanpur, Jonai: Ratanpur, a Mishing traditional village, which is situated on the North Bank of Brahamputra, is only 5 km from Jonai town. This village is well connected by road from Jonai town. A total of 65 families dwell in this village. Each family has its own weaving tradition. The women and young girls are expert in weaving of different colourful Mishing designs. Most of them are self sufficient with their own requirement of clothes like *Makhela Chadder*, *Ri:bi:gasang*, *Mibu Galuk*, *Gamucha* and *Erhi chaddor* etc.

REFERENCES

Indira Gandhi National Centre for Arts (IGNCA, 1999), *Arts & Crafts of North East*. Retrieved from http// :www.ignca.nic.in on 02/03/2004

6

Huge Potential (Conclusion)

The attempt to map the crafts of Assam for touristic consumption has identified the regional pockets of craft concentration. The study also brings out certain traditional villages around these pockets so that the tourists can have a fresh look at the way crafts are being produced in the State. The relationship between communities and traditional knowledge has long been established, and therefore, this relation is exploited while mapping the crafts of Assam also.

The crafts of Assam are unique and have the potential of attracting many inquisitive minds those look for thrill in authenticity and in purity. The craft works of Assam are still genuine and authentic and the magic of modernity has barely polluted them. The natural fabrics too are of huge potential to be promoted as the *main* attraction for the tourists chosen to visit Assam.

Package tours promoting craft tourism along with natural tourism can be of huge success and the craft map produced as a part of this report can work as a catalyst in this regard. In the following paragraphs a brief discussion is offered on some recommended circuits for promoting the crafts of the State. Travel circuits can serve as a foundation of offering package tour.

GOLDEN CIRCUIT

In this circuit the attraction offer golden moments to tourists could be included. This will be a short tour and the tourists could be back in Guwahati in 2 days and 1 night. The following itinerary be taken up for this circuit.

Itinerary for Golden Circuit

	Destination	*Time Required*
Originating point	*Guwahati*	
Stop over	Sualkuchi	3 hours
	Hajo	1 hour
	Sarthebari	1 hour
Over-night halting	Kokrajhar	5 hours
(Visit to adjoining villages)		
Wind up	*Guwahati*	

TEXTILE CIRCUIT

This is a longer circuit than the Golden Circuit as this will touch all the major textile producing regions of the State. The tour thus will crisscross the whole State of Assam. The proposed brief itinerary is as follows. The tour will take 7 days and 6 nights of hectic travelling and sightseeing.

Itinerary for Textile Circuit

	Destination	*Time Required*
Originating point	*Guwahati*	
	Sualkuchi	3 hours
Night halt	Kokrajhar	5 hours (excluding night)
	Nalbari	1 hour
	Dhemaji	5 hours
Night halt	Lakhimpur	1 hour
(River crossing through Khabalughat 22 km from North Lakhimpur town)		
Night Halt	Majuli	1 day
(River crossing through Nimatighat)		
Night Halt	Jorhat	(no visit)
Night Halt	Diphu	1 day
Night Halt	Haflong	1 Day
Wind up	*Guwahati*	

NATURE CIRCUIT

In this package the destinations otherwise famous among tourists are clubbed up with textile and other craft producing regions. One example will be the *Guwahati-Kaziranga-Golaghat-Titabor-Guwahati* circuit. This typical tour will take 4 days and 3 nights to complete.

Itinerary for Nature Circuit (Example only)

	Destination	*Time Required*
Originating point	*Guwahati*	
2 Nights Halt	Kaziranga	1 full day
On way to Titabor	Golaghat	2 hours
	Titatbor/Karanga	5 hours
Night Halt	*Jorhat*	
Wind up	*Guwahati*	

HERITAGE CIRCUIT

In this circuit it is proposed to include destinations famous for heritage of culture and craft. There might be three quick such tours, one for Lower Assam and two others for Upper Assam. In the Lower Assam tour Kokrajhar may be connected with Guwahati, while in the Upper Assam tours Guwahati-Majuli and Guwahati—Jonai may be included. It is needless to say that all the three tours will have intensive rural exposure. The Guwahati Kokrajhar tour may be detailed as follows.

Lower Assam Heritage Circuit (Example only)

Itinerary

	Destination	*Time Required*
Originating point	*Guwahati*	

One point stop	Kokrajhar
Day 1	Saljora village,
Day 2	Ambari Village
Day 3 (morning)	in and around Kokrajhar town and wind up
Wind up	*Guwahati*

These are few examples of clubbing the craft attractions with those of traditionally famous attractions of Assam. The circuits are depicted in a Map 5 for quick and ready reference. However, it is possible to develop tours only on craft work. However, meticulous planning, promotion and executional skills will be required to successfully develop Assam into a textile tourism hub. The dream of bringing in Assam into the mainstream of ***Textourism*** or ***Craft-tourism*** of the world will take a concrete step with the mapping of the craft producing regions which might attract the tourists with a big bang. If successful it will not be impossible to connect Assam with other South East Asian Craft Circuits comprising of Thailand, Indonesia and Vietnam.

A few areas were beyond the scope of this study. Developing tour itineraries ready for execution is one such area.

The promotional campaign including suggestions regarding the print or electronic brochures and other PR materials may entail another detailed study about the regions and their real attractions for different segments of tourists. This is necessary because of the existence of sub-

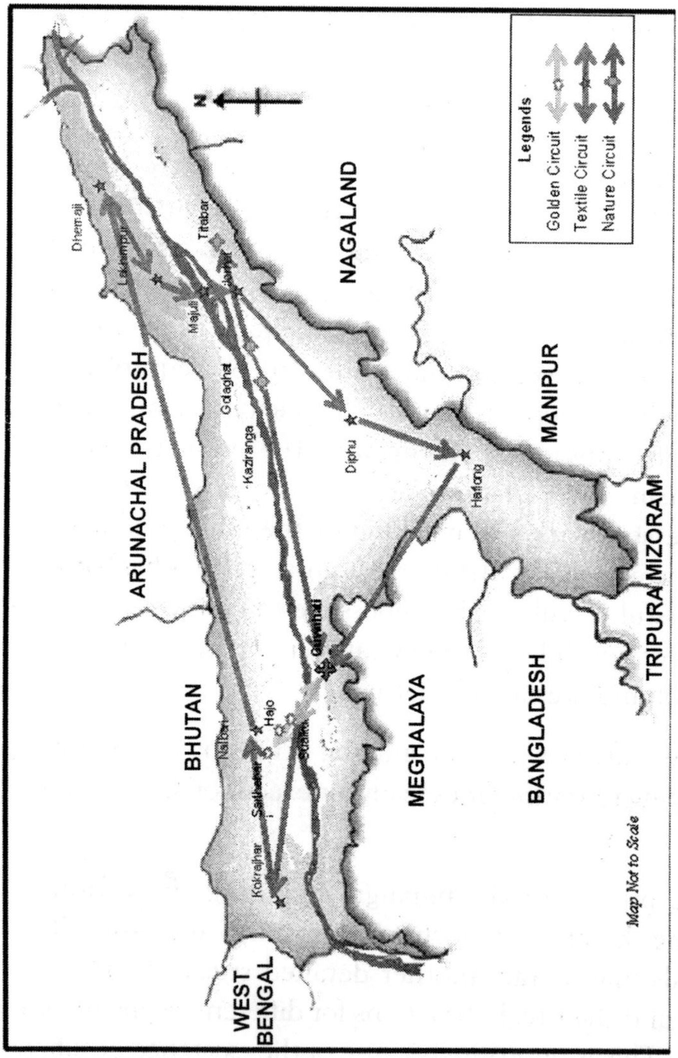

Map 5: Assam—Suggestive Tourist Circuits I

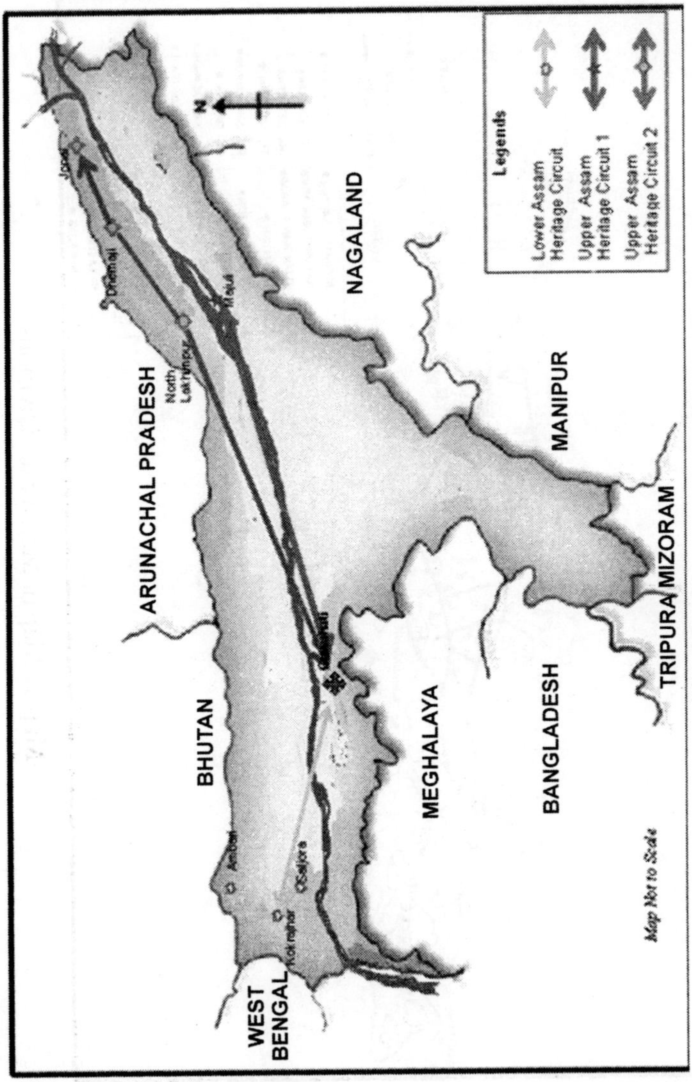

Map 6: Assam—Suggestive Tourist Circuits II

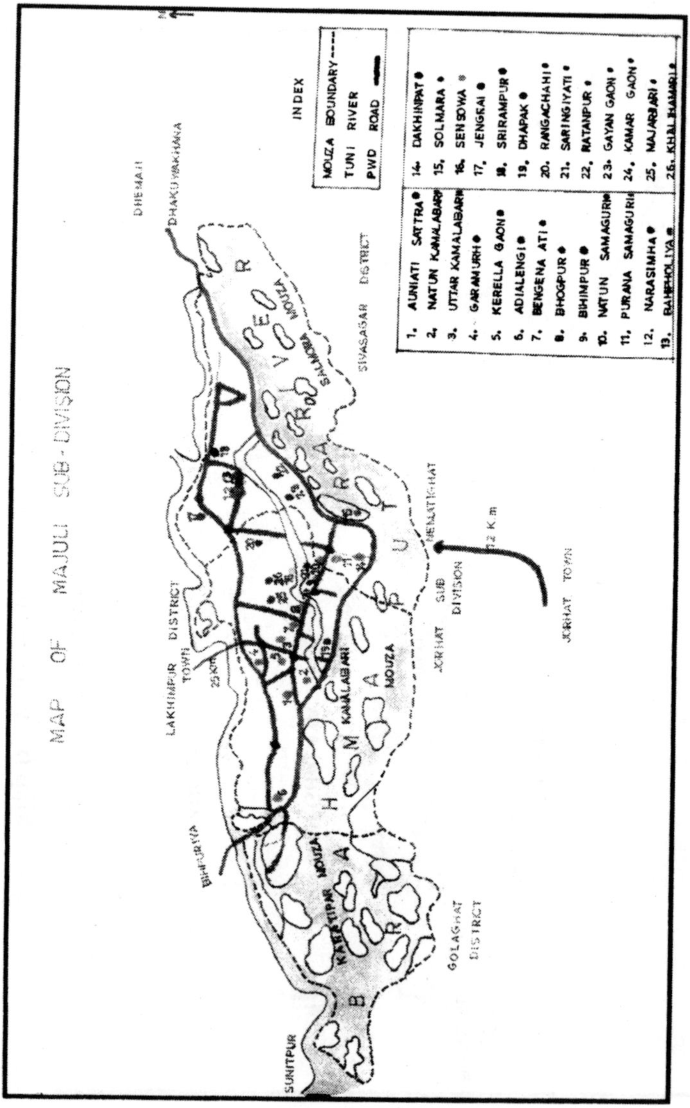

Map 7: Map of Majuli Sub-Divisions

groups among the generalised segments that might be attracted towards heritage or craft tourism. Unless the finer needs are understood by the tour operators, successful planning, execution and resultant production of satisfied customers will be difficult, if not impossible.

Bibliography

BOOKS, MONOGRAPHS, REPORTS

Baruah, S. K. (2004), Tribes of Assam, *Assam Year Book 2004*, Guwahati: Jyoti Prakashan.

Bhattacharyya, P. C. (Ed.) (1962), *Asomor Janajati*, Jorhat: Asom Sahitya Sabha.

Bordoloi, B. N., Sharmathakur, G. C. and Saikia, M. C. (1987), *Tribes of Assam* (Vol. I), Guwahati: Tribal Research Institute, Assam.

Bordoloi, B. N. (1991), *Tribes of Assam*, Guwahati: Assam Institute of Research for Tribal and Scheduled Cast.

Carter, B. W. (2004), Tourists as cultural groups, *Tourist Behaviour* (Ed. A. Raj). New Delhi: Kanishka.

Goffman, E. (1959), The Presentation of Self in Everyday Life, New York: Doubleday.

Gunn, C. (1988), *Vacation Scape*, New York: Van Nostrand Brindhole Company.

Hanks, P. (ed.) (1979), *Collins Dictionary of English Language*, London: Collins.

Harrod, T. (1995), *The Crafts in Britain in the 20th Century*, New Haven, CT: Yale University Press.

Mipun, J. (1993), *The Mishings of Assam*, New Delhi: Gyan Publishing House.

Mishra, S. N. (2004), *Muga Silk Technology*, Sualkuchi: Central Silk Technological Research Institute.

Porananond, P. (2000), Tourism and cultural changes: the crafts of Chiang Mai in M. Robinson, N. Evans, P. Long, R. Sharply and J. Swarbrooke (Eds.), *Reflections on International Tourism. Expressions of Culture, Identity and Meaning in Tourism*, Sunderland: Business Education Publishers Ltd.

Pula, M. L. (2000), *Tribal India: Communities, Customs and Culture*, New Delhi: Dominant Publishers and Distributors.

Sarma, M. K. (2000), Destination positioning of Northeast India based on preferences and perceptions of tourists, Unpublished doctoral dissertation, Tezpur University, Tezpur.

Sengupta, S. (1996), *People of Northeast India*, New Delhi: Gyan Publishing House.

Singh, A. K. (1993), *Tribes and Tribal Life*, New Delhi: Swarup & Sons.

Singh, K. S. (1994), *The Scheduled Tribes*, New Delhi: Oxford University Press.

Smith, S. (1990), Dictionary and Concepts in Recreation and Leisure Studies, Westport, CT: Greenwood Publishing Group.

Waddell, L. A. (1975), *The Tribes of the Brahmaputra Valley*, New Delhi: Logos Press.

ARTICLES

Borgohain, Mamoni G. (2005, February 1), Mishingsakalar hastatat bastrat phular naksha, *Prantik*, 31-32.

Blundell, V. (1993), Aboriginal empowerment and souvenir trade in Canada, *Annals of Tourism Research, 20(1)*, 64-87.

Bezbaruah, M. K. (1999), Tourism—Current Scenario and Future Prospects, *Yojana*, August 8, p. 7.

Bordoloi, B. (1972), Lalung Jatir Parichay, *Ringsang*, 1(1).

Cohen, E. (1988), Authenticity and commoditisation of tourism, *Annals of Tourism Research of Tourism Research, 15*(3), 371-386.

Creighton, M. (2001), Spinning silk, weaving selves: Nostalgia, gender and identity in Japanese craft vacations, *Japanese Studies, 21(1)*, 5-29.

Crippen, Kaye (2000), The threads that tie textiles to tourism in M. Hitchcock and W. Nuryanti (Eds.) *Building on Batik. The Globalization of a Craft Community.* Hants: Ashget Publishing Limited.

De Vidas, Anath Ariel (1995), Textiles, memory and the souvenir industry in the Andes in M. F Lanfant, John B. Allcock and Edward M. Bruner (Eds.), *International Tourism, Identity and Change.* London: Sage Publication.

Gait, Sir Edward (1929), *A History of Assam*, Guwahati: Lawyers Book Stall.

Ghosh, G. K. (1992), *Tribals and Their Culture, Volume I*, New Delhi: Ashish Publishing House.

Godbey, G. and Graefe, A. (1991), Repeat tourism, play and monetary spending, *Annals of Tourism Research, 18(2)*, 213-225.

Healy, Robert G. (1994), 'Tourist merchandise' as a means of generating local benefits from tourism, *Journal of Sustainable Tourism, 2(3)*, 137-151.

Kim, S. and Littrell, M. (1999), Predicting souvenir purchase intentions. *Journal of Travel Research, 38(2)*, 153-162.

Littrell, L. (1990), Symbolic significance of textile crafts for tourists, *Annals of Tourism Research, 17(2)*, 228-245.

Littrell, Mary Ann, Baizerman, Suzane, Kean Rita, Gahring, S., Niemeyer, S., Reilly, Rae and Stout, JaneAnn (1994),

Souvenirs and tourism styles, *Journal of Travel Research 33(1)*, 3-11.

MacCannell, D. (1976), Staged authenticity: Arrangements of social space in tourist settings, *American Journal of Sociology, 79(3)*, 589-603.

Sapir, E. (1924), Culture, genuine and spurious, *American Journal of Sociology, 29*, 401-429.

Sarma, M. K. (2003), Towards positioning a tourist destination: A study of Northeast India, *Asean Journal of Hospitality and Tourism, 2(2)*, 104-117.

Shenhav-Keller, Shelly (1995), The Jewish pilgrim and the purchase of souvenir in Israel in M. F. Lanfant, John B. Allcock and Edward B Bruner (Eds.), *International Tourism, Identity and Change*, London: Sage Publication.

Snepenger, D. J., Murphy, Leann, O'Connell, Ryan and Gregg, Eric (2003), Tourists and residents use of a shopping space, *Annals of Tourism Research, 30(3)*, 567-580.

Timothy, Dallen J., Butler and Richard, W. (1995). Cross border shopping: a North American perspective, *Annals of Tourism Research, 22(1)*, 16-34.

WEB SITES

http://164.100.24.219/rsq/quest.asp?qref=115542 retrieved on 30/01/07.

Indira Gandhi National Centre for Arts (IGNCA, 1999), *Arts & Crafts of North East*. Retrieved from http//:www.ignca.nic.in on 02/03/2004.

Yavary, H. (1992), A glance at Iranian handicrafts, *Hands and Creativity*, (Published by Iran Handicrafts Organisation),

Spring 1992. In http://www.irvl.net/IRAN42.HTM, retrieved on 20/03/2004.

—— (2005), Tourism Statistics for India in www.fhrai.com/mag-news/magTourismStatisticsIndia.htm browsed on 19/12/2005.

World Resource Institute (2003), *Tourism: International Tourism receipts*, Retrieved on 22/03/2004 from http://earthtrends.wri.org/text/ECN/variables/252notes.htm.

World Tourism Organisation (2003), World tourism in 2002: better than expected, *News Releases*, *27/01/2003*, Madrid. Retrieved on 22/03/2004 from http:// www.world-tourism.org/Release/2003/jan/Numbers2002.htm.

World Tourism Organisation (2004), Global troubles took toll on tourism in 2003, growth to resume in 2004, *News Releases*, *27/01/2004*, Madrid. Retrieved on 22/03/2004 from http://www.world-tourism.org/Release/2003/jan/Numbers2003.htm.

World Travel and Tourism Council (2004), *Global Travel and Tourism Poised for Robust Growth in 2004*, Retrieved on 11/03/2004 from http://www.wttc.org/News31.htm.

OTHER WEBSITES

Anya Ek Jagaran, (N.D.). Brochure. Guwahati: ARTFED.

Artfed: Agragatir Ek Khatiyan (N.D.). Brochure. Guwahati: ARTFED.

Bikashar Sopanere (2002), Brochure. Guwahati: ARTFED.

CANEBOO: *Catelogue on Cane and Bamboo*, Guwahati: ARTFED.

Dhubri Hastashilpa Samabai Samity Ltd. (N.D.). Brochure. Dhubri: Dhubri Hastashilpa Samabai Samity Ltd.

Excellence of Handwoven (N.D.). *Brochure, Guwahati: ARTFED.*

Muga Cocoon Drying Centre (N.D.). Brochure. Palashbari: Muga Cocoon Drying Centre.

Roje Eshanshali Cooperative Society Limited (N.D.). Brochure. Kokrajhar: Roje Eshanshali Cooperative Society Limited.

Sheer Magic Unfolds: ARTFED's Handwoven Textiles for the World (n.d.). Brochure. Guwahati: ARTFED.

Silk Map of North East India (N.D.). Sualkuchi: Central Silk Technological Research Institute.

Souvenir (1997), National Handloom Expo. Guwahati: ARTFED.

Souvenir (2003), National Handloom Expo. Guwahati: ARTFED.

Souvenir (2004), National Handloom Expo. Guwahati: ARTFED.

Souvenir (2004), National Handloom Expo. Tezpur: ARTFED.

The Best of Artfed, (n.d.), Brochure. Guwahati: ARTFED.

The Symphony of Dreams and Designs... (n.d.), Brochure. Guwahati: ARTFED.

Unveil Imaginations (2004), Guwahati: ARTFED.

Urvashi: The Galaxy of Assam Handloom from Artfed. (n.d.). Brochure. Guwahati: ARTFED.

Write-ups, Souvenirs, Brochures etc.

www.incredibleindia.com

www.mapsofindia.com

Index